JESUS TAKES
A SIDE

JONNY RASHID

Foreword by **DREW G. I. HART**

JESUS TAKES

A SIDE

Embracing the
POLITICAL DEMANDS
of the Gospel

HERALD
P R E S S

Harrisonburg, Virginia

Herald Press
PO Box 866, Harrisonburg, Virginia 22803
www.HeraldPress.com

Study guides are available for many Herald Press titles at www.HeraldPress.com.

JESUS TAKES A SIDE
© 2022 by Jonny Rashid. Released by Herald Press, Harrisonburg, Virginia 22803.
  800-245-7894. All rights reserved.
Library of Congress Control Number: 2022932199
International Standard Book Number: 978-1-5138-1043-0 (paperback);
  978-1-5138-1044-7 (hardcover); 978-1-5138-1045-4 (ebook)

Printed in United States of America

26 25 24 23 22   10 9 8 7 6 5 4 3 2 1

"In our day and age, it is easy to lose sight of the real Jesus and how we, ourselves, become advocates with him. Jonny Rashid's *Jesus Takes a Side* leads us straight to Jesus and makes clear the path we are to walk with him. Rashid's book is refreshing to read and substantial in content. I enjoyed it immensely."

RANDY S. WOODLEY, author, activist, and co-sustainer at Eloheh Indigenous Center for Earth Justice

"In his new book, Jonny Rashid moves his readers from abstraction and politeness to the place where Jesus stands, waiting to welcome us home. Through biblical interpretation, stories of being a pastor, and his experience as an Arab American, Rashid cuts through fears of conflict and polarization to expose the difficult and beautiful work of the gospel. With prophetic witness and embodied hope, Rashid ignites in readers a faith that draws us all into freedom."

MELISSA FLORER-BIXLER, author of *How to Have an Enemy* and lead pastor of Raleigh Mennonite Church

"In *Jesus Takes a Side*, Jonny Rashid skillfully invites Christians to follow the Jesus who took the side of the marginalized—every time. In an era when being 'nonpolitical' has become a path for many Christians to keep so-called peace, Rashid challenges us to move beyond the temptations of 'bothsidesism' and into lives of prophetic witness. You may not agree with every theological or political position Rashid takes, but make no mistake about it: this book will provoke important conversations about what it means to follow Jesus in any political system. Highly recommended!"

KURT WILLEMS, pastor of Brentview Baptist Church in Calgary and author of *Echoing Hope*

"*Jesus Takes a Side* is almost jarringly political, saying out loud what we tend to talk about among ourselves or, if we're especially brave, write in carefully worded social media posts. Rashid dismantles sacred cows like taking the 'third way,' unity, bipartisanship, consensus and compromise, and 'bothsidesism,' arguing convincingly that they ultimately protect the status quo and don't upset the norms like Jesus did throughout his ministry. Using familiar stories and teachings from Jesus' life, Rashid makes the case that Jesus didn't meet anyone in the middle; there is no third way between the oppressor and the oppressed."

HARRIET SIDER BICKSLER, editor of *Shalom! A Journal for the Practice of Reconciliation* and editor for the Brethren in Christ Historical Society

"*Jesus Takes a Side* reminds readers of the church's central call to liberation that necessitates a resolute stance. This book is for all who are weary from passive centrism that fails to penetrate the gospel's imperative of centering the least of these, which is undeniably political. Jonny Rashid lays to rest amenable quietism while resuscitating Jesus' message of unequivocal preference for society's marginalized in a way that will leave readers empowered and revived."

ROSE LEE-NORMAN, formation pastor at Sanctuary Covenant Church in Minneapolis and adjunct assistant professor of reconciliation studies at Bethel University

"In *Jesus Takes a Side*, Jonny Rashid calls Christians to recognize the political implications of the gospel of the Jesus they proclaim, a politics that centers the marginalized, liberates the oppressed, and calls us to take a side."

MATTHEW THIESSEN, associate professor of religious studies at McMaster University and author of *Jesus and the Forces of Death*

"*Jesus Takes a Side* presents a compelling rebuttal to the tired mantra 'I'm not a Republican or a Democrat—just a follower of Jesus.' This third way politics of neutrality works for the privileged, but wreaks havoc on the marginalized. Rashid draws on Scripture and his pastoral experience to animate a God who sides with the oppressed and who invites the church to do the same. A must-read for ministering to this moment."

DREW STRAIT, assistant professor of New Testament and Christian origins at Anabaptist Mennonite Biblical Seminary

To Elaine, Agatha, Kristen, and also to Circle of Hope

Contents

Foreword

I met Jonny Rashid about ten years ago at the old Infusion Café on Germantown Avenue in Philadelphia. This wasn't your commercial, sterile Starbucks coffee shop; it was a locally owned, small and intimate shop where I knew the regulars and they knew me. It was situated in a racially and socioeconomically diverse neighborhood that defied American segregation's typical patterns. Here worlds collided that wouldn't (and shouldn't), according to those historically in power. I spent a lot of time in this small business as I studied my way through an MDiv program and then eventually pursued my PhD right down the street at Lutheran Theological Seminary at Philadelphia. The day I met Jonny, we had already been in conversation via email, planning for my visit to his church, Circle of Hope, to give a talk on racism and the church. We were getting together to get to know each other better and work out the details for this important gathering and conversation.

I'm not sure whether either of us could have articulated it at the time, but we were each undergoing growing pains in our life journeys that were deepening our commitments to the way of Jesus, requiring us to explicitly take sides with the most vulnerable and oppressed among us. In particular for Jonny, as he'll explain in this book (and I'll say more about in a moment), he was moving toward the full inclusion and affirmation of LGBTQIA people in the church. For me at that moment, the talk I would deliver to his faith community would be my last one with "racial reconciliation" in the title. For several years I had seen how that framework prioritized white Christian comfort over actual justice and liberation for racialized and exploited peoples. That day, we were encountering each other on a journey seeking to align with the Jesus who preached "good news to the poor" and committed to "letting the oppressed go free."

I often joke that moderate and centrist Christians think of themselves as more reasonable and balanced than everyone else. However, their unfaithfulness is exposed when you place the logics of centrism in the context of historical injustice. What does a moderate "third way" mean in the eighteenth-century fight to abolish slavery or maintain it? Or should we go halfsies between the Holocaust and its resisters? Should we meet in the middle in regards to South African apartheid? No, of course not! Yet when it comes to police brutality, white supremacy, economic disparities and exploitation, or many of the other great challenges of our day, many self-professed Christians call for neutrality, moderation, or outright apolitical avoidance.

This is most striking among many neo-Anabaptists, who are frequently inclined toward choosing a centrist "third way" in the midst of two polarized sides. Too often it becomes a strategy that plays things safe with partisanship (Republicans and Democrats) by cutting the issue right down the middle. Ironically, moderate third-way Christians have actually distorted the original meaning of Walter Wink's term. For Wink, passivity toward or accommodation with the powers was not taking the Jesus way seriously. The same went for violent revolution. For him, the third way was nonviolent resistance that explicitly took sides with the poor and oppressed against the powers. The origins of the term are completely lost now because neo-Anabaptists have Columbused the word, and its main appropriation is expressed through political quietism, centrism, and political cowardice. None of these are features of the Jesus story found in Matthew, Mark, Luke, and John.

One of the most striking chapters in this book is Jonny's confessional journey toward full ecclesial affirmation of LGBTQIA Christians in the church. That chapter, and his earlier articulation of his own bodily experience in light of President Donald Trump's "Muslim ban," help the rubber hit the road in terms of why this book's topic matters. If Jonny is right that God is not neutral but instead takes sides with the oppressed and vulnerable (and I can't read the Jesus story and conclude otherwise), then this is a matter of faithfulness. As he says pointedly in chapter 3, "Our goal is to be on *God's side*, not for God to be on ours."

Jonny Rashid is someone I've known for about a decade now. He is a caring pastor seeking to be faithful while pastoring a Philly congregation. Every word of this book is written with this pastoral heart and discipleship focus, even as he challenges the church toward a prophetic imagination and counter-consciousness. His basic premise that the God revealed in Jesus Christ has taken sides with the least, last, and little ones of society requires political courage and ecclesial commitments that align with what God is doing for the poor, the foreigner, the widow, and the orphan. Let these simple yet challenging words change how you show up in the world as we participate in God's liberating and loving presence.

—Drew G. I. Hart

Associate professor of theology at Messiah University
and author of *Who Will Be a Witness? Igniting
Activism for God's Justice, Love, and Deliverance*

Introduction

And I, whose head was girt about with horror,
said: "Teacher, what is this I hear? What folk
is this, that seems so overwhelmed with woe?"

And he to me: "This wretched kind of life
the miserable spirits lead of those
who lived with neither infamy nor praise.
Commingled are they with that worthless choir
of Angels who did not rebel, nor yet
were true to God, but sided with themselves.
The heavens, in order not to be less fair,
expelled them; nor doth nether Hell receive them,
because the bad would get some glory thence."

—Canto III of *The Inferno*, from *The Divine Comedy* [1]

For Christians, it is our duty to take a side, like Jesus has. Through my life and experience, I have come to believe that this is especially important when it comes to making political commitments.

But making those political commitments can be challenging, provoking anxiety, and leading us to second-guess ourselves. All of us—but especially Christians—are bombarded with messages about how conversations about politics are impolite, how we should keep private who we vote for, and in general, how we should not make things about politics.

Faced with the actions of some of the most vocal politically committed Christians—the ones who use the name of Jesus to support White nationalism and White supremacy—political commitments often leave Christians with a bad taste in their mouths. They see the damage that can be done by such bold embrace of politics that harms Christian witness and shy away from the political arena entirely. But it is not commitments, or taking a side, that is the problem here, but rather the side we take. In this book, I confront the myth that Christians shouldn't make political commitments. More than that, I propose that we find our political commitments from our fidelity to God, the one who sides with and liberates the oppressed. "Third way" politics are not an option when Jesus makes it clear whose side he is on.

Because Christian leaders so often value political quietism, this book's message may challenge what some might consider polite and decent. But the stakes of staying quiet, the stakes of not making political commitments, are far greater than impolite conversation or even the discomfort of those who would rather check their politics at the door.

When we remain apolitical in the face of injustice and oppression, we are complicit in harming the "least of these," as Jesus says in Matthew 25. We cannot seek political harmony as an expression of the gospel because the gospel has political ramifications. If we are more concerned with divisiveness than we are with faithfulness, we will end up opposed to God and the oppressed.

In our churches, faithfulness must matter more than political harmony—this is an essential lesson for the American church to learn, and for disillusioned Christians and secular observers to notice. The Christian witness is at stake when we don't take a stand and take a side. We need bold leadership to root out White supremacy and Christian nationalism from our churches and our society. This work demands political participation, not quietism. We need Christians who are convicted to stand against injustice. This book encourages Christians to engage politically, and names that engagement as a matter of practicality, not righteousness. These practicalities are meant to extend the common good. They are not what saves us or what will deliver us, but we must do what we can now as we await our full liberation.

Jesus Takes A Side is for oppressed Christians and their allies who are frustrated by the neutrality and complicity of political quietists. It's for Christians who care about the poor and oppressed (or are themselves poor and oppressed) but haven't felt permission from Christian leaders to engage in a political way to advocate for peace and justice. This book offers a biblical argument for why Christians must engage politically, and practical ways to engage politically, for the "least of these."

If that's you, keep reading. I hope you leave engaged and excited for the common work we are doing together in the name of Jesus for the sake of the least of these, for the sake of the oppressed.

Philadelphia, Advent 2021

Chapter 1

The Politics of My Body

Our church's first love feast after Donald Trump was inaugurated as president of the United States changed me.

Our church celebrates something called the love feast, also known as an agape feast in some traditions. It is a worship meeting where we fellowship and reconcile among one another, letting our love and unity prevail. You can find references to love feasts in Jude and 1 Corinthians[1]. At them, we eat together, welcome new members, and take communion.

At our love feast in January 2017, our team had assigned me to offer the words of institution and the elements of communion to the assembly. Admittedly, my mind was elsewhere. Donald Trump's first executive action as the new president was in effect. We know it colloquially as the Muslim ban, but formally it is Executive Order 13769: Protecting the Nation from Foreign Terrorist Entry into the United States. It was a travel ban against people from a list of Middle Eastern countries and it had gone into effect that Saturday. It barred entry for anyone (with some exceptions) from Iran, Iraq, Libya, Somalia, Sudan, Syria, and Yemen.[2] I got a notice on my phone that there were Arab immigrants in airports and they could not enter into the country because the ban was in effect. My heart sunk. As an Arab-American, it felt like my extended family was trapped there, like I was trapped there. I texted some friends and leaders in the room so they might share in my lament. I was distressed. I was enraged. I was beside myself. I could not believe the worst had happened, even though it is precisely what our new president had said he would do. He began his presidential campaign with this brazenly racist (and false) statement:

> When Mexico sends its people, they're not sending their best. They're not sending you. They're not sending you. They're sending people that have lots of problems, and they're bringing those problems with us. They're bringing drugs. They're bringing crime. They're rapists. And some, I assume, are good people.[3]

It was a clear message to me that I did not belong. And to even the least politically engaged, it was worthy of repudiation. I lamented that so many White Evangelical Christians (81 percent of them, in fact[4]) led him to the White House. And in his inaugural address, Trump doubled down:

> Every decision on trade, on taxes, on immigration, on foreign affairs will be made to benefit American workers and American families. We must protect our borders from the ravages of other countries making our products, stealing our companies and destroying our jobs.[5]

The terms "American workers and American families" explicitly exclude immigrants—people like me. Though he only makes economic points here, the idea of protecting our borders from other countries emphasizes that immigrants are a threat to the livelihood of American workers and families. But Trump was not always as careful, and I knew more institutionalized hatred against immigrants was coming. When it arrived that January weekend, I was not prepared for how much it would hurt me, as a child of immigrants.

All of this was swirling around in my mind as the love feast continued. And then it was time for communion. My heart heavy, I went up to the podium to share the words of institution. But I choked up. I have survived as an immigrant in this country by hiding my emotions and covering my shame. I did not want people to view me as even lesser by seeing how injured I was by my oppression. I only need one hand to count how many times I've cried in public in my ten-plus years of service as a pastor. I was always composed and controlled. But then it happened: tears streamed down my face before I could read the passage in 1 Corinthians. My heart was broken. My people were trapped. I was trapped. So I finally said that I could not offer the meal without mentioning these trapped immigrants. Those immigrants, children among them, looked like me and my children. I felt their strife within me because I have felt it in my life. I know what it is like to not be included, to be left out, just because of how I look and where I am from.

I told the gathered assembly that I needed Jesus to save me again. I needed the communion meal. I needed the reassurance of salvation that was granted to me by a suffering servant, one acquainted with the oppression that I felt as a Brown man in a White country in a predominantly White church. At the same time, I felt comfort as some of our congregation left the love feast to go protest at Philadelphia International Airport. Their protest was part of their worship that night. They took the message of the gospel to the streets, for the sake of the poor and the oppressed.

At that moment I realized once again that the cross of Jesus Christ has an undeniable political connotation. It saves captives. It frees the oppressed. It liberates. It rights all wrongs.

It reconciles the world to God. Jesus dying on the cross is a political event. And the love of Christ it demonstrates compels us to be political, too.

I love how Fleming Rutledge describes the meaning of the cross in her exhaustive book on the subject, *Crucifixion:*

> Forgiveness is not enough. Something is wrong and must be made right. . . . This setting-right is called rectification (*dikaiōsis* in Greek, also translated "justification") by the apostle Paul. . . . When we read in the Old Testament that God is just and righteous, that doesn't refer to a threatening abstract quality that God has over against us. It is much more like a verb than a noun, because it refers to the power of God to make right what has been wrong.[6]

As we shape ourselves like the cross, we also enter into this work of setting the world aright from injustice and deception. This is intrinsically political work. We do it to model Christ, we do it in partnership with Christ, and we do it because we've been transformed by Christ. The salvation of Christ is a worldwide phenomenon that Christians have too often reduced to an individual one. Seen as a work for all people and all of society, the political ramifications of the crucifixion are undeniable.

I knew this, but in that moment I felt it more urgently. As I connected the present political moment to the cosmic political event of Christ's crucifixion, I did so with trepidation. While many Christians will agree that Christianity has political connotations, it is safer to name the cross's politics as transcendent. But Jesus is not merely transcendent, he is also immanent. And in his immanence, in his presence, in his incarnation, he engages the world in all ways, including politically. You can see this clearly in the Gospels, especially around how Jesus engages in the religious-political discourse within Judaism. How Jesus rewrites the Law of Moses in the Sermon on the Mount is one example. The Sermon on the Mount is Jesus' comment on the Law of Moses, on the Torah. Jesus makes it clear that following him is not just a matter of following rules, but living into them. So he intensifies the consequence of the law in the Sermon on the Mount, while also intensifying grace for his followers. We can look, too, to how he engages in political and religious debates and commentary with both the Pharisees and Sadducees, who are both religious and political.

Jesus engages in such a political way because of how society sees him, *and specifically how they see his body*. As a poor, Palestinian, Jewish rabbi, Jesus has skin in the game, you might say. The meaning the society around him offered his body, or his faith, his socioeconomic status, and his ethnicity, was *political*. When I say political, I do not mean related to governance, strictly speaking, but relating to public affairs and matters. Jesus' body has political meaning because it had public meaning. His body connected him to the local politics of first-century Palestine, just as mine does to twenty-first-century United States. The intimate connection Jesus has with his political context is the entire point of God becoming a person, of Jesus being God incarnate, of Jesus embodying God.

While I was conscious of this as I was approaching the pulpit to offer communion, I also knew this was not a common approach to politics and faith. So even though the communion table was not the time or space to make such an argument, I could not let go of what was happening within me. In lieu of a biblical and theological exercise, I put my own body on the line. I shared my personal experience because I could not authentically offer the Lord's Supper without saying what it meant for me in that moment.

I admit I feared I was making my skin color a problem, or at least that I would be accused of such a thing. As I said earlier, love and unity are the expressed reasons for our love feast. Questions raced through my mind: Would a politically-oriented communion meal bring division? Did I have to sacrifice my own dignity for the sake of Christian unity? Is that what Christ was calling me to? What kind of Christianity is that?

I feared that I would be accused of politicizing the moment, or worse, desecrating the table itself. My tears, and vulnerability, would certainly make it unseemly for anyone to make such a critique directly to me, but I still feared what they thought. I had to share what was happening with me if I was going to offer the meal authentically. For me to even partake, I needed to declare Jesus' hope against the evil we had just witnessed.

Even as we partook in communion, I knew that the salvation and liberation that Jesus provided the oppressed didn't take away their plight. It doesn't take away my plight. Those trapped in the airport in that moment were victims of racism, regardless of whether we took communion or not. A racism that had been codified into law.

I was overtaken. I was heartbroken. This isn't ideological, it's personal. It's not partisan, it's embodied. What was happening to these immigrants was happening to me. And then I remembered what Jesus said in Matthew 25. What was happening to these immigrants wasn't happening just to me—it was happening to Jesus, too. Jesus says, "I assure you that when you have done it for one of the least of these brothers and sisters of mine, you have done it for me."

Jesus met me in my distress, because he has felt it, too. Jesus knows the plight of not belonging, of having "nowhere to lay his head" (Matthew 8:20). He knows what it's like to be mocked about where he's from, like when Nathanael mocks

Nazareth, asking the question, "Can anything good come out of Nazareth?" (John 1:46). He feels for the oppressed, he is with the oppressed, because he is one of the oppressed. He brings the oppressed great joy and fills them with good news. He moves us to do the same, as he is one with them (John 17:21). Jesus' arrival in the world signals this. He is born in a marginalized town, Bethlehem (away from the political power center of Jerusalem). He is born of a lowly woman, who praises him for seeking favor with the lowly. The people who first receive this good news are lowly, oppressed shepherds—not political powerbrokers. Jesus' very incarnation roots him and directly connects him with the oppressed.

Throughout the Trump administration, many people thought that my overt political messaging and call to action were a problem for my witness. I heard that protesting Trump's manifestly racist actions was divisive and excluded people. But calls for unity and inclusion that burden the most vulnerable are not unifying or inclusive. They just ask the oppressed to cope with their condition, or worse, to act like it does not exist.

I could not imagine how these Christians—who aren't far-right conservatives, who consider themselves compassionate or committed to antiracism—could see such actions and not be convicted to resolutely repudiate them and comfort those they wounded. I wondered, *Where is your outrage? Are you not witnessing the same evil I am?* For me, it is not a radical political action to repudiate Donald Trump when he calls immigrants animals[7], or when he tells U.S. Representatives to go back where they came from[8], or when he names the countries they are from using derogatory and offensive language[9].

Then I realized that in many cases they could not see what I did because of their own white skin and how it, too, has been politicized. Because those statements don't directly harm them, they can interpret them as merely a different political message. What I can see as a plain moral wrong that demands a strong political response, they see only as politics as usual.

Both my faith and my skin color have formed my participation in politics. I can either deny that reality and be complicit in my own oppression, confront it within myself, or I can do my part to bring to light the dignity through which God sees all of the oppressed, and in doing so invite my Christian brothers and sisters into a fuller understanding of who God is and what the love of God actually looks like.

My experience as an ethnic minority led me to ask questions about U.S. foreign policy after September 11. Not only was I immediately concerned about the domestic treatment of Brown people, I also didn't think bombing them overseas was an expression of the peace and love that I knew from the example and the teachings of Jesus of Nazareth, even when I was in high school. So I couldn't reconcile the Bush administration's invasions of Afghanistan and Iraq because of my growing Christian conviction against war, and also the deeply personal nature of those wars, because they were targeting people who looked like me.

The Obama administration continued the wars that George W. Bush started, using the post-9/11 Authorization for Use of Military Force (AUMF) resolution, even expanding those wars in many ways. In 2016, Obama deployed 26 thousand bombs on seven countries with unmanned aircraft called drones. Obama used ten times the amount of drones than his predecessor did.[10] Obama did this because he was interested in removing American troops from the Middle East, even if that did not mean ending the war. My embodied and lived experience informed my political understanding and reaction to these forever wars, and still does.

For me and my politicized body, the question is not whether to be a quietist, but whether to ignore parts of my lived experience, as if they don't matter, or deceive myself into thinking that they aren't legitimate or important. The necessity of political commitments for me as a person of color does not necessitate partisanship, but it can occasionally *appear* to be partisan. Minorities have a lived experience that informs their faith, and when we are fully dignified and permitted, that experience serves as a witness to Jesus and what his gospel is.

My awareness of how my body has been politicized is only apparent to me because of my lived experience; it does not make my body more political, but simply makes the politics of my body apparent. Again, people of color and other minorities are especially in tune with how their bodies have been politicized because of their lived experience. For people with power, whether they are White or men or a member of any dominant group, they need to learn from the lived experience of minorities, and then, in turn, discern how their bodies have been made political, and how that politicization compels them to act politically. It is uncomfortable to become conscious of that. If we are to live in the fullness of who we are in Christ, we must understand the meaning that our skin color is assigned so that we might consciously live beyond it.

This may not be an easy process for members of dominant groups because it requires them to observe the unearned power and privilege they have collected, and interrogate it. Oftentimes, feelings of defensiveness or denial emerge. I can relate to this as a man, but also as a Brown man. Acknowledging the fact that I had been a victim of racism is incredibly painful to me. I felt that pain accompany me on that Saturday evening in 2017 when I walked up to the pulpit to offer communion, and I feel it every day. I fear that my experience will be questioned;

I fear that I will question it myself since avoidance is much easier than confrontation here. But if I am to live in the fullness of who I am in Christ, I must understand the meaning that my skin color is assigned so that I might consciously live beyond it.

The same is true for people in dominant groups. They do themselves a disservice when they ignore the political meaning that their body is assigned, in order to be apolitical or to be a political quietist. Dominant people then should join in solidarity with people of color and other minorities, people who have been adversely affected by the politicization of their bodies, and work to change the politics of our society. They do this in order to liberate people from their worldly circumstances, so they can enter fully into their new selves in Christ.

This sort of self-awareness and realization may be intimidating and uncomfortable, but as we enter into this difficult work we can—and must—lean on the fact that "there isn't any condemnation for those who are in Christ Jesus" (Romans 8:1 CEB). If we believe that we'll be condemned for interrogating our complicity in the politicization of the bodies of minorities, we will run away from it. But we have freedom in Christ to discern our complicity and repent of it, without fear of condemnation. We can then freely discern how our own bodies have been politicized, without rebuke.

I can only speak for myself as a person of color, but it takes me a lot of courage to name the pain I've experienced and the political action I've taken as a result. So when the oppressed lead you, it is essential to listen and to consider what they are saying. An apolitical Christianity is untenable for oppressed minorities. A gospel that doesn't liberate is no gospel at all. Minorities understand this in a more urgent way than their counterparts. And more than that, minorities need that message to follow Christ, and they understand this truth of the gospel and live it out as an example to the wider church. When we advocate for a Christ without political consequence, we are missing not only the example of Christ, but the opportunity to learn from the experience of his vulnerable followers, the "least of these" whose side he takes every time.

Chapter 2

Jesus Sides with the Oppressed

I first encountered the idea that God sides with the oppressed after reading Black liberation theology in seminary—particularly the work of theologian and thinker James H. Cone. Cone was a widely influential theologian who is considered one of the founders of Black liberation theology. He premises his work on the idea that Jesus came to liberate the oppressed and free the captives, that God sides with the oppressed, and that any gospel that doesn't side with the oppressed is one written by oppressors. Cone writes in *God of the Oppressed:*

> The biblical God is the God whose salvation is liberation. God is the God of Jesus Christ who calls the helpless and weak into a newly created existence. God not only fights for them but takes their humiliated condition upon the divine Person and thereby breaks open a new future for the poor, different from their past and present miseries.[1]

To Cone, Jesus not only becomes one with humanity in his incarnation, but he also becomes one with the oppressed. He not only *sides* with the oppressed, but he also *becomes* the oppressed. The project of Christianity, to Cone, is the liberation of the oppressed. To underline this he quotes Jürgen Moltmann: "The Christian faith not only hopes for freedom but, rather, is itself the inauguration of a free life on earth."[2]

In *A Black Theology of Liberation*, Cone argues that "To understand the historical Jesus without seeing his identification with the poor as decisive is to misunderstand him and thus distort his historical person. And a proper theological analysis of Jesus' historical identification with the helpless is indispensable for our interpretation of the Gospel today."[3]

Cone is making it plain that Christianity is good news for the oppressed, purposed to liberate them. He is saying that a gospel that doesn't liberate is no gospel at all, and that to not understand Jesus as identifying with the oppressed is to not know Jesus at all. These are powerful words, and a strong indictment of other theologies that spiritualize the liberative nature of Christianity. Those theologies reduce our faith to merely offering individual salvation for those who have the right beliefs.

I have to admit, when I first heard this, it threatened my way of thinking about God. Embedded within me is the idea that God is an impartial actor, treating us all the same, regardless of our contexts or lived experiences. This is because I grew up with a theology that saw Jesus as merely an agent for personal salvation via a personal relationship with humans. This gospel is popular in Evangelical churches because people are taught that their personal faith will save them from eternal damnation; fear, then, becomes what motivates them. But this theology is not for the oppressed. The oppressed do not need a threat of damnation to respond in faithfulness. They are already experiencing a form of hell, and they long for liberation. Jesus saves them from their present suffering and promises them a future without suffering.

This is far different than the theology that *threatens* suffering to compel faithfulness. Cone is right. This is the message that compelled early Christians, who were an oppressed minority in whatever culture they found themselves in, to faithfulness. But when the Constantinian influence infused Christianity with imperial power, Constantine brought *prior experience* and *knowledge* about his empire to the text that would make Christianity's adherents, or its magisterial leaders, eschew the fundamental subversive nature of Christianity. Christianity, on its face, threatens imperial powers. So Constantine and the emperors who would follow had to alter how Christians understood their faith in order to maintain their empire.

Howard Thurman asks this question in the preface of his famous work *Jesus and the Disinherited*: "Why is it that Christianity seems impotent to deal radically, and therefore effectively, with the issues of discrimination and injustice based on race, religion, and national origin?"[4] Thurman argues that Jesus' social location was defined by the fact that he was not only a Jew, but a poor Jew, and one who specifically suffered as a minority under imperial oppression.[5]

The event of salvation is then a political event, one that promises liberation through the lordship of Christ. Christianity started as a faith for the oppressed. Early Christians formed alternative communities that resisted the temptations of empire. Most early Christians came from marginal communities, with little access to wealth and power. Their faith further marginalized them. Anabaptists drew upon this example during the Radical Reformation as they resisted the imperial Christianity practiced in Europe. Faced with the temptation to liberate themselves through imperial means, they elected an even more radical reform than their Protestant counterparts.

To Anabaptists, Christianity was only authentic if it reverted to a time before Constantine co-opted the faith as the official religion of the Roman Empire, and made it a weapon of empire. This resistance to empire worked under state churches in Europe, as Anabaptists refused to become citizens via their baptism. They continued the struggle of Jesus against empire. They did so with the oppressed, as the oppressed.

For most European Christians, Christianity at that time was not a subversive religion, undoing the ways of empire, but rather it employed the tools of empire in order to spread the faith and subjugate populations. We can see this clearly during the Crusades, for example, when Christianity was forcibly spread in the Middle East. Imperial European Christianity, whether it was Catholic or Protestant, became a religion *that* oppressed instead of a religion *for* the oppressed.

American Christianity suffered from a different problem, though. Beginning with the first colonists' arrival in the New World, what would become the nascent American empire allowed them more freedom to worship. For Christians in the United States, a focus of political activism has been and continues to be ensuring their own freedom of expression. We see this when Christians advocate for laws that entitle them to discriminate against LGBTQIA folks or deny healthcare that provides for abortions. We see this when Christians ask for the religious freedom to officially celebrate our holidays or display our scriptures on public buildings. It is as if we are pleading with another god (the state) for our liberation and freedom. We can see here the explicit contrast between American Christian theology and the theology that James Cone espouses, or even the theology that early Anabaptists did. Here's how Stanley Hauerwas put it in *After Christendom*:

> Because Christians have been so concerned with support-
> ing the social and legal institutions that sustain freedom of
> religion, we have failed to notice that we are no longer a
> people who make it interesting for a society to acknowledge
> our freedom. . . . We thus fail to remember that the question
> is not whether the church has the freedom to preach the
> Gospel in America, but rather whether the church in Amer-
> ica preaches the gospel as truth. . . . Freedom of religion is a
> temptation. . . [that] tempts us as Christians to believe that
> we have been rendered safe by legal mechanisms.[6]

To build on Hauerwas's argument, when it is the state that
liberates us and frees us by providing us a legal space to worship,
it takes the teeth out of a gospel and a Lord whose purpose is to
liberate and free us. It's important to note that the freedom the
state offers here is freedom to worship, so long as that worship
does not disrupt the order of the state. The state is freeing us by
giving us something that God has already promised. Freedom
of religion no longer makes our faith an agent of change, and
it begs the question of whether or not the church can say no
to the state. It turns our faith from one that stimulates us to
action, like an amphetamine might, to one that sedates us, as
the opiate that many critics of religion have claimed it to be.
Freedom of religion appeases us in satisfaction with our political circumstances because the state has distributed to us our
right to worship in exchange for our loyalty. We can no longer
oppose the state because we have entered a relationship with
it in order to avoid being persecuted by it. This transactional
relationship compels us to not engage politically against the
ones who are purveying our rights.

Hauerwas says, "'Jesus is Lord' is not my personal opinion; I take it to be a determinative political claim."[7] Central to
Christianity is the kingship and lordship of Jesus. This makes

our faith fundamentally political, and it causes our faith to have a political consequence. In fact, he says, "For fifteen hundred years Christians thought Jesus' lordship meant they should rule the world. . . . Some Christians look with nostalgia on the past seeking ways to recapture Christian dominance of the world."[8] I believe we find their American counterparts among Christian nationalists that have had a recent resurgence in the United States. The revolution of the church "was absorbed and subdued. . . the gospel was made a captive to the mechanism of the state."[9] Both American Christianity and European Christendom subdued the political consequence of our faith. American Christianity as it stands is an augmentation of the American experience, merely accessorizing it but never challenging it.

If all the gospel does for you is offer you a promise of personal salvation as you live in the largesse of empire or the dominant system, it fails to have its full meaning expressed. The oppressed then are, simply by virtue of their social position, more in line with God's will for the world and the implication of the gospel, because they need the gospel to matter. If Christianity means freedom, if Christianity means liberation, then we must consider the circumstances we must be freed from, and those who are especially burdened by those circumstances. Here's how James Cone explains what the lordship of Christ means:

> What is striking about the New Testament names of Jesus is the dimension of liberation embedded in them. For example, Jesus Christ as Lord, a postresurrection title, emphasizes his complete authority over all creation. Everything is subject to him.[10] The Lord is the "ruler," "commander," he who has all authority. If "Jesus is Lord," as one of the earliest baptismal creeds of the church puts it, then what does this say about black and white relationships in America?

The meaning is perhaps too obvious for comment. It means that whites do not have authority over blacks. Our loyalty belongs only to him who has become like us in everything, especially blackness. To take seriously the lordship of Christ or his sonship or messiahship is to see him as the sole criterion of authentic existence.[11]

What Cone does that Hauerwas fails to do is name the consequence of the political meaning of the gospel: "Jesus is Lord" means we are liberated from other lords—including empire. This doesn't seem like a difficult statement to agree with on its surface, but what Cone says, and what I also am saying, is that Christians act in accordance with the gospel when they allow the experience and the liberation of the oppressed to inform their politics. God has sided with the oppressed, and an oppressed person is who Jesus becomes. Oppressed people hew closer to God and God to them, not because of anything inherent in them but because for them the gospel becomes the source of actual liberation. They need to be saved.

Christians from dominant groups often do not understand this need for salvation with the same kind of urgency that oppressed groups do. But they aren't at a dead end. Empathizing with the oppressed can change our urgency and even show us the ways that we are oppressed and in need of saving. Whether we learn how we are oppressed, or how we are complicit in oppression, the gospel is good news for all of us because it liberates us all.

The biblical witness showcases that God sees the oppressed, and that God's action in the world is consistently to free the oppressed and to fill the oppressed with "good things," as Mary says when she glorifies God at the annunciation (Luke 1:53).

What's important to note about God's particular covenant with Israel—through Abraham, to whom God makes a covenant and promises a nation—is that it shows that God *favors* people who have not collected their own might and power, but rather have trusted in God. God assures Abraham a nation of his own. God cares for that nation, which is not mighty relative to the empires that surround it, and by doing so, showcases God's particular provision and care for the lowly and the poor.

But God's care for the lowly and poor is not limited to Israel: when Abram and Sarai demonstrate power over someone, namely Hagar, God still protects Hagar. Hagar is Sarai's Egyptian slave, whom she offers to Abram to sleep with in order to reproduce. This violates the covenant God made with Abram because God assured him children, but Abram's impatience prevails. Hagar's pregnancy changes the power dynamic between her and her master, Sarai. She blames Abram for her plight, and Abram says to her, "'Since she's your servant, do whatever you wish to her.' So Sarai treated her harshly, and she ran away from Sarai" (Genesis 16:6 CEB).

Delores Williams, a womanist theologian,[12] says that in running away "Hagar becomes the first female in the Bible to liberate herself from oppressive power structures." Williams continues, "Courageous though her liberation action may be, Hagar is without the support and physical sustenance a pregnant woman needs."[13] The Lord's messenger (which is another way of saying the Lord) meets Hagar in the wilderness, and instructs her to go back to Sarai and "put up with her harsh treatment of you" (Genesis 16:9 CEB). The Lord's messenger offers her a promise, similar to the one that God offered Abram, that Hagar would have many offspring and a nation of her own (Genesis 16:9–11).[14] Here we see again that God shows particular favor to the oppressed, giving the same treatment to this Egyptian slave as God does Abram. Furthermore, Hagar will go on to name the Lord *El-Roi* (Genesis 16:13), which means "the God who sees me." The name she gives God perfectly summarizes her experience with God: God saw her, noticed her, cared for her, as God does for all the oppressed. Hagar is the first person to give God a name, showcasing again the *proximity* which the oppressed have to the Lord. Because of her need for liberation, Hagar had such an intimacy with God that she named God.

Hagar emerges again in chapter 21 of Genesis. In this account, we see that the situation between Hagar and Sarah is as fraught as it is in chapter 16 (vv. 9–10).[15] God emerges again to speak to Abraham and reassures him of the promise God made to him. But in this account, God reassures Abraham that Hagar and Ishmael will be given a great nation as well. Abraham sends Hagar away with minimal sustenance. This is in contrast to her running away in chapter 16 (21:14).[16]

God meets Hagar once again in the wilderness after the meager resources Abraham provided runs out. She openly weeps, knowing that she and her son may succumb to death. God comforts her with the reassurance that God will bless her with a nation. God follows through. Hagar maintains her autonomy by having her own nation, and her freedom by being untethered from Abraham and Sarah. Moreover, she is the one who finds Ishmael his wife, and in doing so she subverts patriarchal norms.[17] God then liberates Hagar and Ishmael from their enslavers and provides them with material resources and a legacy all their own. God sides with the oppressed here in this narrative. God is a redeemer and a liberator.

Grace, as the freedom that Paul talks about, is a comfort because it's hard for those of us in privileged positions to see God on the side of the oppressed, or perhaps taking a side that is not ours. And so we listen to marginalized voices to make this discernment.

Chapter 3

On God's Side

Our goal is to be on *God's side*, not for God to be on ours. To see this, let us consider a story that is familiar for many of us, and that will help us see whose side God is on and allow us to enter into it. For the Israelites, the event that truly bound them together as a people was the Exodus. The Egyptians had enslaved the Israelites. Through the liberation of the Israelites, God adds to the chosen nation.

After Joseph, a favored Israelite patriarch in Egypt, faded from memory, Pharaoh attempted to repress the growth of the Israelites but failed. They strengthened in numbers and Pharaoh oppressed them further into slavery. Eventually, he instructs the midwives to throw every boy into the river in order to further repress the population (Exodus 1). Here we see the necessity of oppression in order for individuals to have power over others. Oppression is a *condition* that is created, and it is those who are subject to it that God favors.

Moses's mother saves her boy, famously, by putting him in a straw basket down the Nile. He is raised among the Egyptians, but remains loyal to the Hebrew people. So much so that he kills an Egyptian who is abusing a Hebrew. But eventually, his murder is discovered and he flees. "Then Moses was afraid and thought, 'What I did must have become known'" (Exodus 2:14 NIV).

Moses sees an injustice, takes matters into his own hands. But his actions are discovered, so he runs away. But his passion for justice, for the oppressed Hebrew people, is what motivates him. This part of the narrative foreshadows what follows. God summons Moses through a burning bush to free his people. God says, "I have indeed seen the misery of my people in Egypt. I have heard them crying out because of their slave drivers, and I am concerned about their suffering" (Exodus 3:7 NIV). God sends Moses to free his people, and through Moses and Aaron, God demonstrates power and supremacy over the people that oppressed his people. God shows this through miraculous actions performed by Moses and Aaron, and through plagues that mock the Egyptian gods (including a plague on the first-born, reminiscent of Pharaoh's own actions that started this ordeal), demonstrates God's own dominance. Pharaoh refuses to submit until finally, when God kills all of his firstborns, human and livestock, he relents. The Israelites plunder the Egyptians, taking back what the Egyptians had stolen from them through slavery. They then celebrate the Passover meal, and start making their way through the Red Sea. Pharaoh and his army regret relenting and pursue the Israelites into the sea. But God "jammed the wheels of their chariots so that they had difficulty driving" (Exodus 14:25 NIV) and the sea topples on them. God's justice prevails and God's people are free.

In Exodus chapter 15, Miriam breaks out into song, celebrating the might of her God, the one who crushed those who opposed and oppressed her. The refrain of this song:

> I will sing to the Lord,
>   for he is highly exalted.

Both horse and driver
    he has hurled into the sea. (Exodus 15:1 NIV)

Some of the dramatic imagery in this story might be uncomfortable for some of us. How could God kill all of Pharaoh's armies? And how could God do so by jamming their wheels into the sea's floor? It seems brutal and merciless. This retributive violence of the Old Testament, particularly found in the books that follow Exodus, is essential to understand in order to hear the yearnings and cries of the oppressed, and also in order to understand how God makes things right. Here, God is besmirched both by the actions of Pharaoh and by the fact that God's people are oppressed. And something must be done about that. Ultimately, that will lead us to the cross, where God's final act of redemption occurs, but that truly is a subject for another book.

Engage your discomfort, should you have it, with the story. And wonder to yourself, Do you see yourself as the Israelites or the Egyptians in the story? Are we ones longing for freedom, or fearful of retribution for our complicity in oppression? Furthermore, this song that Miriam sings is one of an oppressed person, praising God for freeing her. This story that Israel experienced is one that comforts them throughout the ages, as they continually suffer oppression and captivity. It is the heartbeat of the nation, one that is told every year at Passover. They remember that God delivers them and will deliver them once again. It is for this reason that enslaved Black people in the United States remembered the Exodus, to remember God's deliverance.

It is in this same spirit that Jesus of Nazareth comes, promising liberation to his people, and to many more. Right when his birth is announced in Luke 1, Mary, the one who will birth her own liberator, bursts into song. A song that is familiar, in a sense, quite like Miriam's song, comes from her. I imagine Mary was feeling rather like Miriam that day, knowing that she was birthing her own liberator, as she suffered under captivity. The Magnificat demonstrates the favor God has with Mary and the oppressed. Mary says yes to God because she longs for a savior, because she needs a savior, and she knows that God will deliver her. So she joins in song, along with Miriam.

> He has shown strength with his arm.
>> He has scattered those with arrogant thoughts
>>> and proud inclinations.
>> He has pulled the powerful down from their thrones
>>> and lifted up the lowly.
> He has filled the hungry with good things
>> and sent the rich away empty-handed.
> He has come to the aid of his servant Israel,
>> remembering his mercy,
> just as he promised to our ancestors,
>> to Abraham and to Abraham's descendants forever.
>> (Luke 1:51–55 CEB)

When the birth of Jesus is announced to the shepherds in Luke 2, we hear a similar refrain about Jesus bringing peace and goodwill, but specifically to those he favors, those whose side he takes, the oppressed. Even the choice to announce his birth to the lowly shepherds (who probably weren't even watching their own sheep and who had very little rights of their own) shows that God's favor rests with those who desperately need liberation. The famous chorus that the Angels were singing in that sky while shepherds watched their flocks: "Glory to God in heaven, and on earth peace among those whom he favors" (Luke 2:14 CEB).

When we get to chapter 3 of Luke, we see John the Baptist, the radical prophet from the wilderness, quoting the prophet

Isaiah, showcasing once again what Jesus is going to do, what he will inaugurate.

> A voice crying out in the wilderness:
>   "Prepare the way for the Lord;
>   make his paths straight.
> Every valley will be filled,
>   and every mountain and hill will be leveled.
> The crooked will be made straight
>   and the rough places made smooth.
> All humanity will see God's salvation." (Luke 3:4–6 CEB)

Then Jesus himself, when he announces his ministry for the poor and for the oppressed, also reads from Isaiah, fulfilling his prophecy:

> The Spirit of the Lord is upon me,
>   because the Lord has anointed me.
> He has sent me to preach good news to the poor,
>   to proclaim release to the prisoners
>   and recovery of sight to the blind,
>   to liberate the oppressed,
>   and to proclaim the year of the Lord's favor.
>   (Luke 4:18–19 CEB)

Following God and following Jesus has political implications. At the very least, it means Christians must side with the oppressed. God does not take a third way between oppressor and oppressed; God favors the oppressed. Even in the case of Hagar, when she wasn't God's chosen one, God provided and cared. With the Israelites in Exodus, God chose the side of the oppressed. When Jesus arrived, it was clear that he was here to liberate the poor and oppressed. God doesn't elect a third way.

I think what motivates the proponents of third way thinking is that God's "favor" is often not with them. This position is rather unusual for them since proponents of third way thinking so often end up in the dominant position. But because their social locations demand a different understanding, they invent a view of God that does not challenge their social locations. Their fear lies in the fact that there may not be a place in the kingdom of God for the powerful, for the wealthy, for the oppressor. The question the powerful ask is this: If God is for the oppressed, is God for me?

Perhaps the better question is: Are you for God? Will you be on God's side? Will you take the side of the oppressed? What does that mean for your life and your political commitments? What will it cost you and what are you willing to renounce as belonging to God, not to you?

The table of Jesus at his banquet is open, and everyone is invited, but it will cost some of us more to attend. I think we see this clearly in the Bible, too. In the parable of the great banquet, Jesus tells the story of a certain man who wanted to fill his table with guests. He invited people far and wide. When the time of the banquet arrived, he sent his servant to announce that the banquet was ready. But all of his invited guests were too busy:

> One by one, they all began to make excuses. The first one told him, 'I bought a farm and must go and see it. Please excuse me.' Another said, 'I bought five teams of oxen, and I'm going to check on them. Please excuse me.' Another said, 'I just got married, so I can't come.' (Luke 14:18–20 CEB)

What follows is fascinating. The master then turns to the streets to fill his table. He sends his servant to invite guests who are available for his banquet. "Go quickly to the city's streets, the busy ones and the side streets, and bring the poor, crippled, blind, and lame." Who is welcomed at the table of the master? Those who have a vacancy that must be filled, those who are empty, those who are hungry, those who are longing for invitation, acceptance, and fulfillment. Put another way, the oppressed.

Consider the excuses of those who rejected the invitation. They had bought a farm and needed to take care of it. They bought livestock and were preoccupied with that. One person was preoccupied with their marriage, even. All of these things are indications of status, wealth, and position: their material preoccupations prevent them from seeing that they too need liberation. Or perhaps they see the cost clearly and find it too high. We can vividly see the cost of the kingdom of God in Luke 18 and 19. In Luke 18, Jesus is approached by a wealthy ruler who asks him what he must do to attain eternal life. Jesus responds by telling him to follow the laws that the rich man has known for his whole life: "Don't commit adultery. Don't murder. Don't steal. Don't give false testimony. Honor your father and mother" (Luke 18:20 CEB). When the rich man said he had kept those commands since he was a young boy, Jesus added one more:

> When Jesus heard this, he said, "There's one more thing. Sell everything you own and distribute the money to the poor. Then you will have treasure in heaven. And come, follow me." When he heard these words, the man became sad because he was extremely rich. (Luke 18:22–23 CEB)

I think Christians have generally spiritualized this passage to take away its material implications. It is a hard saying for the wealthy to hear directly, so it's understandable to take some of the teeth out of it, so to speak, but the disciples hearing Jesus' interaction with this man took it rather literally. For them, it was as consequential as it is for us. Jesus says that it's easier for a camel to go through an eye of a needle than for a wealthy person to enter the kingdom of God. His disciples respond with "Then who can be saved?" The text continues, "Jesus replied, 'What is impossible for humans is possible for God'" (Luke 18:26–27).

So for the powerful and the wealthy, this passage is indeed weighty, but so is the cost of following Jesus. Jesus doesn't mince words about this. The invitation to be on God's side, or to be at God's table, is for everyone, even if the cost is great. But it is not futile because of what happens in Luke 19. Drew Hart juxtaposes Luke 18 and 19 to showcase the differences between Jesus' call to the table.[1]

In Luke 19, we hear the story of Zacchaeus, a diminutive tax collector who has defrauded many people. He wants to see Jesus so he climbs a tree. Jesus sees him and insists on entering his home. Jesus engages in table fellowship with someone whom the crowd thought was a sinner. However, through that relationship, Zacchaeus is transformed. He leaves the meal ready to repair the damage he has done. Zacchaeus responds with, "Look, Lord, I give half of my possessions to the poor. And if I have cheated anyone, I repay them four times as much" (Luke 19:8 CEB). Hart says:

> This is a powerful liberative story that contrasts radically with the rich ruler encounter. Zacchaeus voluntarily practices a Jubilee ethic through two distinct actions. First, he recognizes that he has a responsibility to all the people living in poverty. Half of his possessions will be given to people living in poverty. Secondly, Zacchaeus understood that his wealth was accumulated through exploitation and by harming those who already had a foot on their neck by an unjust system.[2]

It could have had a much different outcome, however. Jesus instructed his disciples, when they were sent to preach the gospel, to enter into people's homes who welcomed them, to eat with, bless, and heal them. Jesus tells his disciples to say "God's kingdom has come upon you" (Luke 10:9 CEB). Jesus instructs his disciples quite differently, if the people don't welcome them:

> Whenever you enter a city and the people don't welcome you, go out into the streets and say, "As a complaint against you, we brush off the dust of your city that has collected on our feet. But know this: God's kingdom has come to you." I assure you that Sodom will be better off on Judgment Day than that city." (Luke 10:10–12 CEB)

"God's kingdom has come *to* you" instead of "*upon* you." Jesus' words are distinct and powerful. Not even the city's dirt is worthy to be on the sandals of the people who rejected his disciples. Jesus adds to his condemning language that it will be better for Sodom (a city God destroyed after Abraham couldn't find a single righteous person in it—Genesis 19:29) on Judgment Day than it will be for the town that rejects his disciples. It is worth noting that the sins of Sodom are exactly the ones I am talking about here. Ezekiel compared the sins of Sodom to the sins of Jerusalem, "This is the sin of your sister Sodom: She and her daughters were proud, had plenty to eat, and enjoyed peace and prosperity; but she didn't help the poor and the needy" (Ezekiel 16:49 CEB). This is Christian living, this is faithfulness to God. It's what James calls true devotion, "to care for orphans and widows" (James 1:27).

Jesus' warning to the towns who reject his disciples are not unlike the ones in the parable of the great banquet. He says to the individuals who rejected his invitations, "I tell you, not one of those who were invited will get a taste of my banquet" (Luke 14:24 NIV). Jesus is promising judgment and wrath on those who refuse the invitation to the table, who will not

welcome him peacefully. God's will is for every valley to be
filled, and every mountain lowered. The question for us is if
we want to participate in God's will. Regardless of whether we
elect to participate, because it is God's will, we will be compelled to at some point. But joining in God's liberation and
redemption movement now is an invitation into a full life, one
of cooperation with the one who will save the whole world.

Serving the least among us is serving God. We will be
judged by our response to this call. In Matthew 25, an apocalyptic text, Jesus warns that those who don't feed the hungry,
clothe the poor, welcome the stranger, and visit the prisoner,
have failed to serve God. He says, "I assure you that when you
have done it for one of the least of these brothers and sisters of
mine, you have done it for me" (Matthew 25:40 CEB).

God stands on the side of the oppressed. Jesus refuses to
take a third way between oppressor and oppressed. He meets
no one in the middle. Everyone is invited to the table; however,
for the powerful among us, the invitation comes with a cost.
For everyone, the invitation is liberation, which the oppressed
already welcome. The oppressors, however, must risk surren-
dering everything to take Jesus' side.

Chapter 4

"Why Do You Have to Make Everything So Political?"

That's a question I've been asked on more than one occasion, from people wondering whether I could just check my politics at the door instead of making politics an issue at the dinner party, at the cell meeting, or during Sunday worship. Politics is so often reduced as secondary to human relationships that many consider it inappropriate or rude to bring it up in polite company. What they find polite is the idea of being nonpartisan, or appearing nonpartisan.

But apoliticality is not truly possible. Politics inform our existence, and rejecting politics as a subject matter, as if it were merely a topic for impassioned discussion, allows the politics that infiltrate our society to go unchallenged and unnoticed. The powers that be, the ones who control political power and constrain political imagination, benefit when we consider politics an impolite topic for conversations and regular interactions. And more importantly, as we have seen, the good news of Jesus has economic and political consequences that require a faithful response. We cannot settle for being polite when truth—and the gospel itself—is at stake.

Politeness, itself, is often about vanity. Social norms and customs are all designed for assimilation, adapting into society, and when we break those rules, we are named as disrupters and rabble-rousers—and who wants to be known for that? We don't want people to be upset with us, and politics is something that has the potential to elicit those kinds of strong feelings. As an immigrant to the United States, I had to learn the rules of this country to fit in, and one of those rules is to keep politics out of polite discussions. The status quo in the United States is dependent upon making politics an impolite topic. If you bring it up at the dinner table, you are the one causing problems. For many Americans, it is easy enough to avoid politics with their acquaintances and even friends. Politics is generally a boring subject, and the powers that be want to keep it that way.

But 2016 changed all of that. Trump disrupted "politics as usual" and awakened people to the reality that politics is connected to everything. Unsurprisingly, the 2020 election turned out the highest percentage of registered voters in over a century.[1] The intensity of people's political engagement increased because the stakes of our politics were finally clear to all. Politics became particularly *existential* during this time, a matter of our existence. Everything increasingly became politicized and political. Or rather, was revealed to be what it always was.

We often heard about how polarized our world was, and that polarization was portrayed negatively. I think a better explanation is that we recognized how political our world was all along. Ordinary people, whose lives were previously not impacted by political results and outcomes, began to engage in politics because they saw clearly, perhaps for the first time, that politics and political commitments do matter.

Radical language is meant to provoke and deepen resentments. Just as some people became politically engaged in opposition to Trump's racism, other people also became politically engaged because Trump's racism validated their own. Long gone was the compassionate rhetoric of yesterday's politicians. To see the change, look at how Ronald Reagan and George Bush described immigrants in the 1980 Republican primary. Asked about undocumented people attending high school, here's Bush:

> "I'd like to see something done about the illegal alien problem that would be so sensitive and so understanding about labor needs and human needs that that problem wouldn't come up. But today if those people are here, I would reluctantly say they would get whatever it is that their society is giving to their neighbors."

Reagan added:

> "I think the time has come that the United States and our neighbors, particularly our neighbor to the south, should have a better understanding and a better relationship than we've ever had. And I think we haven't been sensitive to our size and our power."[2]

The statements from the candidates are hardly benign, but they aren't full of vitriol and hatred. In terms of *rhetoric*, they appear, at least, to be crafting a narrative about decency and compassion, and even self-awareness.

But Trump's campaign disrupted how we engage in politics, and it befuddled commentators. This put some pastors and churches in a difficult position, especially those who had largely avoided overt politics in their messages and congregations.

Before the 2016 election and especially during the Obama administration, the church I serve made it a hallmark of its theology to attempt to transcend the political binary of Republicans and Democrats. We were hardly apolitical, but we believed in a sort of radical politics that removed us from making overt political commitments. To us, both the Democrats and the Republicans were racist, capitalist warmongers. We were able to transcend partisanship by essentially naming both sides as problematic.

This *can* offer us a path toward a radical following of Jesus, but it can also lead to a tepid moderate position. For us, it seemed fairly harmless to stick to our convictions about peace, compassion, and nonviolence, and equally vilify both sides of the political spectrum. It made us *appear* both nonpartisan and not of the world, and generally scratched our justice-oriented people where they itched. They could talk about the radical way of following Jesus because it was a clear affront to both sides of the political spectrum. When we're dealing with Mitt Romney and Barack Obama, I can see the reason to hold such a position. We do not need to be overtly political because politics is seemingly, at least rhetorically, constrained to a certain framework.

But all of that changed in 2016 when Trump bore the fruit of the increased radicalization of the Republican Party. The Republican Party's obstinacy and recalcitrance occurred well before Trump. This polarization may have started in the Reagan eighties, when lines were drawn and both sides grew more ideological than they were in the seventies and sixties, when you can see more broad coalitions, even relating to issues of civil rights and the environment. But after Reagan, that polarization worsened under Bill Clinton and George W. Bush. Historians suggest a variety of reasons for that polarization, including diversity, income inequality, geographic distribution, and so on.[3] But even during Obama's time, he witnessed a strong reaction to his own *person*. Here's how Obama described how he experienced this polarization:

> When I started running in 2007–2008, it was still possible for me to go into a small town, in a disproportionately white conservative town in rural America, and get a fair hearing because people just hadn't heard of me. . . . If I went into those same places now—or if any Democrat who's campaigning goes in those places now—almost all news is from either Fox News, Sinclair news stations, talk radio, or some Facebook page. And trying to penetrate that is really difficult. It's not that the people in these communities have changed. It's that if that's what you are being fed, day in and day out, then you're going to come to every conversation with a certain set of predispositions that are really hard to break through.[4]

Why did the polarization increase so notably under Obama, when the chasm had been growing for decades before him? Obama blames the news media's pummeling of information that personal relationships cannot transcend. I believe the nation itself struggled to handle a Black president, and we saw racist vitriol thrown against Obama, especially surrounding his place of birth, following his election. What the racism against Obama shows us is not something new in our political arena, but rather something that was always there, and put into plain view because of Obama's skin color. The hatred against Obama ultimately gave way to Trump's White supremacy.

As Christians, we can and must demonstrate moral courage in the face of evil, and we can do so without waiting for the worst forms of racism to show themselves. We can do so because we relate to Jesus, and he authors our political courage—one that sides with the poor and the oppressed, with the outcast and the marginalized, with the least of these siblings. We can prophetically speak because we are related to the One who grieves even before the worst of who we are is revealed.

American Christianity, too, suffers from a lack of will to make the truth plain when lies are apparent, and to name racism as what it is. We serve the state's commitment to framing U.S. democracy as salvific when we engage in the same failure to name evil and truth plainly. It infects our churches and our pastors. While there are many examples of Christians actively supporting White nationalism, anti-immigrant rhetoric, and racism, in general many Christians see the apparent evil but are paralyzed in responding. We are fearful of appearing partisan, which I think we have been taught both by the aforementioned media, and also by the rhetoric invoked by Donald Trump.

It is often our vanity that leads us to worry about appearing partisan when truth and justice are on the line. If we are committed to being truth-tellers, then our failure to speak clearly about the truth for fear of being labeled partisan makes us liars. But it is better to tell the truth, and be named partisan, than to avoid that label and continue to deceive others.

Jesus is much more concerned with the fruit we bear than with our appearances. The writer of the gospel of Mark delivers this clearly when he puts a story of a cursed fig tree before and after the clearing out of the temple in Mark 11. A hungry Jesus approaches a fig tree that is full of leaves—in other words, one that appears to be in season—and when it bears no figs, he curses the tree. "He said to it, 'May no one ever eat fruit from you again'" (Mark 11:14).

The writer of Mark sandwiches this story (a strategy often employed by this writer in order to draw comparisons) around the cleansing of the temple. Jesus enters the temple and overturns the tables of the money changers, who were selling sacrifices with an inflated exchange rate, and he drives them out. He effectively "cursed" the temple in the same way that he did the fig tree. After this occasion, Peter notes that the fig tree Jesus cursed had withered. Jesus then expresses that he is much more concerned with outcomes than appearances.

This teaching not only convicts those who want to appear nonpartisan in order to seem peaceful or unifying; it also convicts people who try to say the right things, but act otherwise. Surely most people wouldn't explicitly endorse racism or violence, but if the *outcomes* or the fruit of their work doesn't express that, they are like a fig tree full of leaves that doesn't bear fruit. So yes, almost everyone decries the idea of racism, but when we are faced with an opportunity to do something about it, so many stall because they don't want to appear political, which ultimately means they fail to *act righteously.*

This theme emerges in Matthew when Jesus is lamenting the hypocrisy of Jewish leaders, whom he expected to ally with and be close to in his ministry. They appear pure on the outside—Jesus even calls them beautiful—but the outcomes of their work, which show what is happening on the inside, are what matter most. They are not unlike Christians who want to appear peaceable, polite, and kind—because they never bring up politics at the dinner table or a church small group meeting or from the pulpit—but because their outcomes, their fruit, don't bear peace, they reiterate the violence of our world.

Jesus says they "neglect the weightier matters of the law: justice and mercy and faith," effectively straining "out a gnat but swallowing a camel." Jesus doesn't think politeness is unimportant, but reminds us that if we sacrifice justice, mercy, and faith in its pursuit, we are hypocrites. He goes on to say they are concerned with the appearance of cleanliness "outside of the cup and of the plate, but inside they are full of greed and self-indulgence." Jesus, on the other hand, is much more concerned with the inside of the cup being clean, which will in turn clean the outside. For Jesus, and for us, care for the poor and meek in our politics is essential, even when prioritizing and advocating for these needs makes us appear political. Finally, he intensifies his critique, calling the hypocrites "whitewashed tombs," on the outside looking beautiful while their outcomes, and their insides are, "full of the bones of the dead and of all kinds of filth." They look "righteous to others," but inside they are not righteous at all (Matthew 23:23–28).

For American Christians, an appearance of holiness can often be equated with not appearing political or partisan, or not politicizing a circumstance. Sometimes we can posture ourselves as if we are above such political matters, and reduce Jesus to a pacifying figure, as if Jesus does not care what happens to his children. Jesus teaches us that appearances of holiness should not be our focus at the expense of holiness itself. Jesus was distraught that as he was working to bring a new order to the world, what he called his kingdom, he was blocked by people more concerned about appearing righteous than about bringing forth actual righteousness and justice. It reminded me of what Beto O'Rourke said to CNN about a mass shooting in West Texas that left seven dead:[5]

> The rhetoric that we've used—the thoughts and prayers that you just referred to—it has done nothing to stop the epidemic of gun violence to protect our kids, our families, our fellow Americans in public places. . . If we don't call it out for what it is, if we're not able to speak clearly, if we're not able to act decisively, then we will continue to have this kind of bloodshed in America, and I cannot accept that.[6]

In the full quote, O'Rourke uses profanity to make his point even more forcefully. Say what you will about O'Rourke's foul language, but in the face of mass shootings, he knew it was more important to rebuke the violence than to watch his tongue and maintain his decorum. Sometimes it is more important to clean the inside, so to speak. That is the point Jesus is making: that appearing "presentable"—or in this case, apolitical—is less important than standing up for truth and justice.

Jesus names the necessity of a commitment to truth as a commitment to him. In John 18, Jesus tells Pilate he came to testify to the *truth*, something the media suffers from not doing. Here's a brief section of the correspondence between Pilate and Jesus: Pilate asked him, "So you are a king?" Jesus answered, "You say that I am a king. For this I was born, and for this I came into the world, to testify to the truth. Everyone who belongs to the truth listens to my voice." Pilate asked him, "What is truth?" (John 18:37–38a).

Jesus demonstrates his commitment to unwavering truth, and Pilate, the governor who is interrogating him and will go on to sentence him to death, wonders what truth is. Pilate longs to wash his hands clean of this conflict between Jews, but he can't, and he will be responsible for it.

How do Christians enter into this space? Since we answer to a different Lord, other than the "lord of objectivity," we can name that we are explicitly biased in favor of truth and in favor of love, both of which are antithetical to lies and racism. And in fact, many Christians did that very thing when White supremacists rallied in Charlottesville, Virginia, in 2017 and following the rally, where clergy took a stand against the far-right groups.

Cardinal Daniel DiNardo, president of the United States Conference of Catholic Bishops, described the events at

Charlottesville as "abhorrent acts of hatred." Cardinal Blase Cupich directly responded to Trump's comments: "When it comes to racism, there is only one side: to stand against it." Russell Moore, who formerly led the policy branch of the Southern Baptist Convention called the Ethics and Religious Liberty Commission, said "the so-called alt-right white-supremacist ideologies are anti-Christ and satanic to the core."[7] These Christians, who do not represent the progressive left by any means, demonstrate clear speaking about the matters of race and racism, especially when it was so reprehensible. But we mustn't wait for the most wicked version of racism and hatred to rear their heads to speak the truth.

It is more faithful to name the truth plainly, as opposed to making our truth cater to "both sides." Not only does this make us, as Christians, resist the patterns of this world, but it makes us the truthful prophets we need to be. The impulse for Christians to "both sides" every argument is one we have collected from the world, where the truth is not often stated plainly. The reason I point out the worldly nature of this perspective is that it is often maintained because its proponents errantly believe that they are resisting the world by refusing to take a side. But it is worldlier to be so lacking in boldness or assertiveness when it comes to telling the truth. And that's what this is about.

Jesus demonstrates his commitment to this truth in Luke 11 when he visits a Pharisee and doesn't wash his hands. It is similar to the cleansing motif in Matthew 23, but here, Jesus makes the political and material stakes even clearer:

> While he was speaking, a Pharisee invited him to dine with him; so he went in and took his place at the table. The Pharisee was amazed to see that he did not first wash before dinner. Then the Lord said to him, "Now you Pharisees

clean the outside of the cup and of the dish, but inside you are full of greed and wickedness. You fools! Did not the one who made the outside make the inside also? So give for alms those things that are within; and see, everything will be clean for you." (Luke 11:37–41)

The Pharisee rebukes Jesus for not cleaning his hands, and Jesus responds that the ceremonial cleaning, while not unimportant, certainly doesn't eclipse the more important matters of the law. Jesus names their concern about the law as hypocritical and superficial. He does not name the law as such, but rather, their lack of concern with righteous outcomes of it. Jesus instructs them rather plainly to gives alms to the poor, thereby expressing the cleanliness of the inside of their hearts and lives. The *outcome*, the *fruit*, bears witness to our character more than our appearances. Jesus' lack of concern with appearances later results in his death, so there's no shortage of consequence for bold political and prophetic proclamation. At the end of his Seven Woes to the Pharisees, Jesus accepts his fate as someone whom his beloved Jerusalem would stone. He longed to disciple Jerusalem, but because of their unwillingness:

> "Jerusalem, Jerusalem, the city that kills the prophets and stones those who are sent to it! How often have I desired to gather your children together as a hen gathers her brood under her wings, and you were not willing!" (Matthew 23:37)

Jesus' life is a warning for all bold prophets: when you do not operate by the rules of society, you are risking your livelihood, or perhaps even your life. In our case today, following the rules of society means being apolitical—not bringing politics up and not making things political. However, in being apolitical we are certainly risking the lives of the ones we do not advocate for. When Jesus' disciples declare his lordship upon his entrance to Jerusalem in Luke 19, they cause such a commotion that the ruling religious leaders ask Jesus to have them quiet down. Jesus says, "I tell you, if these were silent, the stones would shout out" (Luke 19:40).

Jesus' point is simple: if Christians do not advocate for the oppressed out of fear of appearing partisan, political, or offensive, others will; even the stones will cry out. We will see bold prophets around us doing the work of God, and perhaps we won't recognize them as Christians, because our faith has been so watered down to the point of having no material significance. If our faith fits nicely into our political economy, it consequently does not disrupt it. Yet we know that Jesus' disciples were disrupting their political order when they greeted their Lord during his triumphal entry:

"Blessed is the king
    who comes in the name of the Lord!
Peace in heaven,
    and glory in the highest heaven!" (Luke 19:38)

The disciples of Jesus resolutely make a political statement and cause a political disruption by worshiping another king besides Caesar. This of course leads to the death of Jesus, but prophets must take risks for the sake of God's truth and God's justice. The pursuit of truth and justice is far more important than appearing apolitical simply to accommodate our society's norms for polite life—the cross is a testament to this disruptive truth. Too often fear disrupts our pursuits of truth and justice, however.

The fear exists because we want to be polite, we don't want to offend someone, and if we are in the business of selling newspapers, we don't want to upset our profit margins. We are living in a time where the truth, be it about someone's lies or their racism, is seen as an insult. We see it as polarizing. We can't take a stand because we must accommodate all sides, but it is not God who is compelling us to do that, it is the world. So instead of telling the truth, we skirt it, to be polite or appear loving. God has another way for God's followers.

The Bible showcases a different kind of posture. The prophets of the Old Testament identified their concerns with God's concerns, as Abraham Joshua Heschel put it.[8] That is to say, they feel what God feels about God's people and nation, and deliver God's feelings to the kings. One clear example of this is when Nathan rebukes David, the king of Israel, the one after God's own heart, when he murders Uriah after he rapes Bathsheba (2 Samuel 12). Nathan delivers a direct address to David, naming his sin against God, Israel, and Uriah:

> Why have you despised the word of the LORD, to do what is evil in his sight? You have struck down Uriah the Hittite with the sword, and have taken his wife to be your wife, and have killed him with the sword of the Ammonites. (2 Samuel 12:9)

Nathan names the evil as plain, directly confronts David for his crime, and declares that he despises the Lord. David is not faithful to God because he seeks more than what God provided him with. He uses God's enemy to kill one of God's own, and rapes and abducts his wife too. God chose a side, that of the nation of Israel, and David opposed that side to pursue his own interests. Nathan demonstrates the prophetic nerve the church needs in the face of a confounded media and evil administrations. That is the radical call of following God. We aren't meant to always appeal to both sides, but rather, to appeal to God's side. When truth and love are on the line, we must name the lies and the racism. When the world is confused about what is true and what isn't, Christians must lead the effort to declare the truth, without fear.

Chapter 5

Faithfulness Requires Courage

As a pastor, I have experienced it over and over—whenever we start talking about taking a firm stance on an issue, whether it is related to LBGTQIA inclusion and dignity, antiracism, or otherwise siding with the oppressed, we hear about divisiveness.

But the Bible writers do take division seriously; we can see this clearly in in the opening of Paul's epistle to the Corinthian church:

> Now I appeal to you, brothers and sisters, by the name of our Lord Jesus Christ, that all of you be in agreement and that there be no divisions among you, but that you be united in the same mind and the same purpose. (1 Corinthians 1:10)

Paul is making it clear that unity in mission and focus for churches is paramount, and that they should not be divided, specifically by fidelity to different leaders—but rather, united by fidelity to Jesus and his mission. In chapter 12, Paul showcases how to express this unity in the body:

But God has so arranged the body, giving the greater honor to the inferior member, that there may be no dissension within the body, but the members may have the same care for one another. If one member suffers, all suffer together with it; if one member is honored, all rejoice together with it. (1 Corinthians 12:24-26)

Paul's vision for unity in Corinth, and otherwise, is to give greater honor to the oppressed and poor members. Doing so ensures that there is no division of dissension in the body. Paul has a vision for radical egalitarianism and names that as the key to unity in the church. This is a significant contrast from those Christians who suggest antiracism and LBGTQIA inclusion are divisive—far from it, these are the things that bring *unity* to our body. If being faithful to God's call to side with the oppressed is divisive or changes the integrity of the institution or the country, perhaps division is what we need.

In U.S. politics, we have seen this temptation to mistake the appearance of unity at the expense of true transformation in the battle over the filibuster. This rule, which allows the opposition party to stall non-budgetary legislation unless there is a sixty-vote supermajority, was created in 1806 when the Senate realized there was no provision to end debate and force a vote. Before the Civil War, it was used to defend slavery, and then later to defend segregation. It stopped anti-lynching laws and blocked bans on discrimination in housing. The filibuster was the "Southern weapon of choice" against civil rights legislation. More recently, it has been used to stall two pieces of legislation designed to make voting safer and easier, end gerrymandering (a process that allows state legislators to draw the lines for districts, no matter how partisan), reform campaign finance, and expand voting access and transparency when local bodies change voting laws.

Current debates over abolishing the filibuster have been stalled by two conservative Democratic senators, who have defended the filibuster on the grounds of encouraging deliberation and dialogue to move a divided nation toward unity. But if not all people have fair and legal access to voting, that cannot be true unity.

For those who are committed to faithfully following Jesus as advocates for the side of the oppressed, the journey will require courage, because we will be met with accusations of hatred and divisiveness, even and perhaps especially when we are actually resisting those very things. We will be told we hate deliberation and dialogue when we are just trying to get more people to the table. But *faithfulness* is our call, not avoiding conflict or difficult conversations.

This is not to say divisiveness is only or always harmful in the church, in our organizations, or in our country. But it is important to name faithfulness and transformation as the way to unite us all, rather than merely ignoring our differences and the power between them. In her book *How To Have An Enemy,* pastor Melissa Florer-Bixler asks this question: "Who defines the center of our identity, one that pushes aside questions that are considered divisive politics by some but are life or death to others?"[1] She notes that those in power are the ones who tend to name what is divisive and what is not, even if it comes at the expense of the most vulnerable. For Florer-Bixler, "Power separates difference from enmity."[2] And it is the powerful who are leading us into being divided, while those of us who resist do so for the sake of our lives.

When we do try to build unity without transformation, we burden the oppressed specifically, asking them to deny their livelihoods for the sake of "unity." But a body that is united through the debasement of minorities should not stay united—that is not true unity. When Jesus sent his disciples to ministry, he expected confrontation and division, and in fact said that he was not coming to bring peace at all. Jesus knew this because of his impending death, and he knew his disciples wouldn't be treated any better: "If they have called the master of the house Beelzebul,[3] how much more will they malign those of his household!" (Matthew 10:25).

> "Do not think that I have come to bring peace to the earth;
> I have not come to bring peace, but a sword.
>> For I have come to set a man against his father,
>> and a daughter against her mother,
>> and a daughter-in-law against her mother-in-law;
>> and one's foes will be members of one's own household.
>> Whoever loves father or mother more than me is not worthy of me; and whoever loves son or daughter more than me is not worthy of me; and whoever does not take up the cross and follow me is not worthy of me." (Matthew 10:34–38)

In this passage, Jesus drew on the prophet Micah to name how the prophecy he brings, the kingdom he brings, will disrupt the very families that we are in. He adopted the Roman *paterfamilias* structure to describe the new household he is creating with his disciples, where he is the master, yet he also acknowledges that this new family structure will fundamentally disrupt the order of the world. In that sense, Jesus was being intentionally divisive. He knew that the aim of his ministry wasn't to create a peaceable religion that neatly fits into the world's status quo.

So when in the Sermon on the Mount Jesus calls us to love our enemies—a teaching that is too often abused to *keep the peace*, instead of to *make peace*—he is asking us to invite them into transformation, into a new way of living. In the passage,

Jesus says that when someone slaps you on the right cheek, turn and give them your left cheek (Matthew 5:38–40). In this illustration, Jesus turns a backhanded slap—a way that an oppressor demeans someone by claiming ascendency over that person—into an openhanded slap. That openhanded confrontation changes the power arrangement in the relationship and is sure to draw even more ire from the oppressor, as they are faced with their power falling flat.

Here's how Howard Thurman says it in *Jesus and the Disinherited*:

> Sincerity in human relations is equal to, and the same as, sincerity to God. If we accept this explanation as a clue to Jesus' meaning, we come upon the stark fact that the insistence of Jesus upon genuineness is absolute; man's relation to man and man's relation to God are one relation. . . . In the presence of an overwhelming sincerity on the part of the disinherited, the dominant themselves are caught with no defense, with the edge taken away from the sense of prerogative and from the status upon which the impregnability of their position rests. . . . The experience of power has no meaning aside from the other-than-self reference which sustains it. If the position of ascendancy is not acknowledged tacitly and actively by those over whom the ascendancy is exercised, then it falls flat. . . . Instead of relation between the weak and the strong there is merely a relationship between human beings. A man is a man, no more, no less. The awareness of this fact marks the supreme moment of human dignity.[4]

Thurman is saying that when we accept our God-given sincerity—that is to say, the fullness of our humanity—we take away the dominator's power over us, because it relies on demeaning someone else. There is no more weak or strong. A person is a person, and that's it. That sincerity changes, disrupts, and divides the power dynamic in our society. This threatens those who have power, and they will go to great lengths to stop it. This led Jesus to his death, and it led Martin Luther King Jr. to his.

On February 1, 1968, a torrent of rain covered the city of Memphis, but the city required its sanitation workers to continue working in the rain. As it rained, two Black men, Echol Cole and Robert Walker, took cover in the back of a garbage truck, where the compactor is. There was an electrical malfunction, and the compactor crushed them to death. The public works department did nothing in return to compensate their families. In response, 1,300 Black sanitation workers went on strike to protest the city's "horrible working conditions, abuse, racism and discrimination."[5] Eventually, Martin Luther King caught wind of the protest and joined in. The spirit of the protest was captured in the signs the men were carrying—in the spirit of Thurman's words above, the workers demanded to be seen as equals, in all sincerity. The protest signs simply read: "I am a man."

The city was obstinate and refused the demands of the workers. The workers were eventually forced to return to work, and some did, but many resisted. After weeks of resistance, on March 28, there was another protest, and it became violent when a group of protesters began to throw objects. A sixteen-year-old protester was killed by police during this encounter. But the protest continued, and King was blamed by officials and the media. A few days later, King gave his last speech, one that essentially foreshadowed his death:[6]

> Well, I don't know what will happen now. We've got some difficult days ahead. But it really doesn't matter with me now, because I've been to the mountaintop. And I don't mind. Like anybody, I would like to live a long

life—longevity has its place. But I'm not concerned about that now. I just want to do God's will. And He's allowed me to go up to the mountain. And I've looked over, and I've seen the Promised Land. I may not get there with you. But I want you to know tonight, that we, as a people, will get to the Promised Land. So I'm happy, tonight. I'm not worried about anything, I'm not fearing any man. Mine eyes have seen the glory of the coming of the Lord.[7]

The next day, a shot rang out, and King was killed on the balcony of the Lorraine Motel. King knew the cost of his protest—he knew his life was at stake. He knew Jesus was serious about the cost of following him.

While it is hardly a surprise when faithful action is named as divisive, King's example reminds us that faithfully following Jesus can upset people to the point of violence and death. It agitates our oppressors. So when we take sides with the oppressed and are named as divisive, we should take that as a sign we are doing the right thing. We are disrupting a system that needs to be disrupted. King is an essential figure to consider here because he is so widely revered in American society. Almost no one would name King as anything but a hero or a modern-day saint. Yet the media at the time named King as an agitator. While King has an 89 percent approval rating today, according to a YouGov poll, in 1966, he had a 67 percent *disapproval* rating.[8] He was unpopular for the same reason that those who side with the oppressed today are: he disrupted the status quo of society. We should expect the same treatment when we follow Jesus faithfully.

Jesus knows that following him, and seeing ourselves as he sees us, causes a massive disruption in society, in organizations, in countries, in families. He knows the cost of following him is high. Even our families, our careers, our livelihoods will change as we journey with Jesus. So we can expect conflict, oppression, and hatred when we do so—not peace. In Luke 9, where Jesus is calling his disciples into ministry, he again makes the high cost of following him clear:

> "Follow me." But he said, "Lord, first let me go and bury my father." But Jesus said to him, "Let the dead bury their own dead; but as for you, go and proclaim the kingdom of God." Another said, "I will follow you, Lord; but let me first say farewell to those at my home." Jesus said to him, "No one who puts a hand to the plow and looks back is fit for the kingdom of God." (Luke 9:59–62)

Jesus' call to follow him is fundamentally disruptive and divisive. We should heed Jesus' warning, knowing that faithfully following him will result in a disruption of our society. Any meaningful change will disrupt the order of things, and tremendous distress and anxiety will follow. When Jesus is addressing his disciples at the end of his life in the gospel of John, he says that when they follow him, they will be hated and persecuted, just as he was. Because they are joining a new family, they will necessarily leave their old one (John 15:18–25). When we name the racism in our nation and in our churches, we'll be accused of dividing the nation or the church, as being unloving and unkind, as mistreating our oppressors. But there is great hope in this—Jesus encourages his disciples at the end of the discourse to "take courage," because he has "conquered the world!" (John 16:33).

Jesus is more concerned about our faithfulness to his mission than the integrity of the world's systems of power and oppression—which are the very ones that will be divided when we follow Jesus. Jesus' mission is powerful and disruptive. He is not concerned with division, and in fact expects it. With this in mind, we must then consider why the apostle Paul warns so much about division.

Throughout the Pauline epistles we see that Paul's ministry is oriented toward including non-Jewish people, or Gentiles, into Christianity. In the Gospels, Jesus speaks very clearly that his mission is only to the sheep of Israel (Matthew 15:24), even as he occasionally ministers to and includes Gentiles. For Jesus, though, Gentiles, pagans, or foreigners are symbolic of people cast out of the fold (Matthew 18:17). Paul essentially reiterates this chronology of going to the Jews first, then second to the Gentiles in the opening chapter of his epistle to the Romans (Romans 1:16). Paul's mission is to make Christianity inclusive of both Jews and Gentiles. In Romans 11, Paul describes this inclusion as grafting new branches onto an olive tree, one that will eventually graft the whole world onto it.

We first get a glimpse of this in Acts 10, where we witness the first Gentile conversion to Christianity. Luke, the writer of Acts, tells us that Cornelius—a Roman centurion and a Gentile—feared God with his household. He offered alms to the poor and prayed to God. The outpouring of this love, the prayer and alms specifically, was an act of worship to God, which God named as a memorial. Cornelius's acts indicated a clean heart, a purified heart.

At the same time Peter, the disciple of Jesus, had a vision from God that permitted him to eat both clean and unclean animals (a significant change from the Jewish law). When Cornelius's servants arrived to invite Peter to come to Cornelius's house, Peter hosted them overnight before setting out, and he ministered to them, explaining that "God shows no partiality" (Acts 10:34) and inviting them into the fellowship. A sort of Gentile Pentecost followed, during which, like Pentecost in

Acts 2, the Holy Spirit descended on the group of gathered Gentiles, and through this Gentiles were given entrance into the church.[9]

Acts 15 describes the meeting of the first ecumenical council of the church, at which the council concluded that they did not need to burden Greek converts with anything other than "that you abstain from what has been sacrificed to idols and from blood and from what is strangled and from fornication" (Acts 15:29). Jewish law requires circumcision. But now uncircumcised Gentiles are included in the fellowship. This was a dramatic and significant shift. The covenant that God offered to Abraham in Genesis was symbolized by circumcision, yet in Acts a radical change occurred for the sake of inclusion. Paul's concern is simple: when the church is not inclusive, it is divisive.

Eventually, even some of the guidance affirmed at the council of Jerusalem changed, though, as Paul seemingly permitted people to eat food sacrificed to idols (see Romans 14 and 1 Corinthians 8). Paul was working on creating an inclusive church where everyone belongs. Paul did not instruct Jewish people to no longer observe their customs; rather, he instructed them not to impose those beliefs on others. We can see this when Paul circumcised Timothy, a man born from a Greek man and a Jewish woman (Acts 16). We also see this when Paul didn't circumcise Titus (Galatians 2:3). Paul, then, values customs, but rebukes imposition of them.

Paul's ire is drawn most strongly when his inclusive mission for the church is compromised. This is what he named as divisive. Right after the council of Jerusalem, a sharp dispute between Paul and Barnabas led to their division. Luke tells us it was a conflict about how they related to a disciple named John Mark,[10] who accompanied Barnabas to Cyprus, while Paul and Silas went to Syria and Cilicia. Paul, however, expounds on the conflict in Galatians 2:

> But when Cephas came to Antioch, I opposed him to his face, because he stood self-condemned; for until certain people came from James, he used to eat with the Gentiles. But after they came, he drew back and kept himself separate for fear of the circumcision faction. And the other Jews joined him in this hypocrisy, so that even Barnabas was led astray by their hypocrisy. But when I saw that they were not acting consistently with the truth of the gospel, I said to Cephas before them all, "If you, though a Jew, live like a Gentile and not like a Jew, how can you compel the Gentiles to live like Jews?" (Galatians 2:11–14)

Paul was incensed that Peter, whom he called Cephas, refused to eat with Gentiles when the "circumcision faction" arrived. Other Jewish people followed him, and the church that was supposed to be inclusive turned into one of division. The unifying mission of Paul is disrupted by Peter's apparent prejudice. Calls for unity that sideline marginalized voices are not actually unifying. Our unity as Christians should be pursued with the marginalized in mind.

Paul also speaks of division in the church when he directly references how wealth and resources were not widely distributed among the people in Corinth. This violated the ethos of the church, especially the church of Jerusalem. At its founding, Luke tells us that the church "would sell their possessions and goods and distribute the proceeds to all, as any had need" (Acts 2:45). In Acts 4 we learn that "no one claimed private ownership of any possessions, but everything they owned was held in common." Furthermore wealth was "distributed to each as any had need" (Acts 4:32–35). This ethic was so strong that the only record of smiting in the New Testament is in the next chapter, Acts 5, when a couple colluded to sell their land and not give the proceeds back to the church entirely. God struck them down, dead! God wanted to be Lord of their money-bags as they distributed among the church. Paul followed this example in Corinth.

In 1 Corinthians 11:18–22, he named the problem of divisions in the church, taking issue with the fact that they were not partaking in the Lord's Supper at all. Why weren't they? Because they did not eat in common, and they all went off to eat on their own. But worse, some hungry people did not get the food they needed, and wealthy people got more than their fair share to the point of drunkenness. He claims that they "look down on God's churches and humiliate those who have nothing" (1 Corinthians 11:22 CEB). That is what he named as divisiveness. He then offered the words of institution and concluded with a sobering judgment on the church, that whoever consumes the Lord's Supper without "discerning the body, eat and drink judgment against themselves" (1 Corinthians 11:29). What is divisive and what is deadly then is oppression, not justice, not inclusivity, not love. Here's how Melissa Florer-Bixler puts it in *How to Have an Enemy*:

> Paul asks the people in this community to conform their eating times and practices to workers and slaves—people who are on the far margins of power in Roman society. Paul can see that the wealthy are using their freedom in Christ, the freedom from belief in idols, to rationalize their division. But liberty isn't everything. Love is.[11]

Paul strongly rebuked the Galatians when he argued that they were using the freedom Christ gave them for self-indulgence, as opposed to service to one another (Galatians 5:13–15). He called them "foolish" for how they were dividing one another up, specifically around the issue of circumcision and requiring it for the wrong people. He says in chapter 5, "For in Christ Jesus neither circumcision nor uncircumcision counts for anything; the only thing that counts is faith working through love" (Galatians 5:6). And he rebuked the agitators suggesting otherwise rather colorfully, wishing they would "castrate themselves" (Galatians 5:12).

In Philippians 3:2 Paul called the people excluding Gentile converts "dogs," "evildoers," and "mutilators of the flesh." His harsh rebuke was reminiscent of Jesus' assertiveness when he says he came to bring the sword and not peace. The reordering of the world that can happen in the church when no one has need and all people are seen as fully dignified is what unites us. Threats to that are divisive.

Paul is serious about divisiveness, that is certain, but he never compromises faithfulness to God for the sake of unity. A unity that burdens the oppressed is a false unity. It is a direct affront to a God who is on the side of the oppressed. It contradicts the vision of Jesus, one that radically reorders the world.

We can expect conflict, division, disruption, and even death if we are heeding the call of Christ. But a politics that sides with the oppressed is the kind of transformative politics that can unite us. It is that common mission that keeps us together. If we insist on prioritizing our unity over that common mission, we will be burdening the most vulnerable, a disobedient act that demonstrates hatred toward God as a willful opposition to God's priorities.

Chapter 6

The Lie of the Third Way

I was sitting in a webinar about how to resolve conflict in our polarized time, and the leader of the seminar referred to the *third way* as a term and an idea that could help us move through our intractable differences and collaborate in a mutually beneficial way. For churches and organizations that are stuck between the poles of sales and operations, or between expansion and investment, or even for a family debating whether to order pizza or tacos for dinner, developing a way to compromise and collaborate for mutual ends is important. The idea of a third way between intractable positions is good, in theory.

The conversation in the webinar moved to a story about someone overserved at a party sharing their opinion that the country they lived in should not welcome more immigrants or refugees. Others thought the country should. As you might guess, the presenter at the webinar described both of these positions as intractable and argued for a third way approach. In this case, the approach was rooted in empathizing with both sides and imagining an alternative that the presenter insisted wasn't a compromise, but rather one that they could agree on. On one hand, the presenter argued, the person who opposed immigration was thinking of self, and the ones in support of immigration were thinking of "the other."

I spoke up in the discussion and named plainly that in a dialogue about whether to accept immigrants or not—one where the poles are "self" and "other"—I was lost. The people discussing welcoming immigrants were discussing welcoming *me,* and those who were talking about excluding immigrants were discussing excluding *me.* I was the "self," in the side that was caring for the "other."

In this discussion, a third way approach is only possible when the politics at hand are abstract. For White citizens of a Western country, the politics of immigration are *fundamentally* abstract, because they aren't affected personally. But the politics of immigration deeply affect me. My position may indeed seem intractable, but it is only intractable insofar as my politics are embodied. It is intractable because I will always be myself, and no amount of creativity can change that. The discussion then is not *ideological* but *existential* for vulnerable minorities.

I asked the presenter, "In my case, what does one do? How does a third way approach work for me?" The presenter argued that I could separate my ideas from my body. In other words, I could remove some of the pain I experienced when someone suggested people like me shouldn't be allowed in the country. But distancing myself from the politics of my body is a dehumanizing prospect. And the work to remove politics from someone's body, to assure them it's possible, or that their bodily trauma is indeed merely a psychological condition (or an intellectual one), can be abusive. My strong, intractable as some would say, feelings about immigration are rooted in my lived experience, and distancing myself from them would be distancing myself from my humanity.

In conversations where bodies are on the line, some have suggested that those most personally affected should remove themselves from the dialogue because it may be too intense for them. But the idea that the dialogue should happen between those who are least affected decenters the experience of those who are most affected and further abstracts the discussion, which can lead to both harm and erasure. The most affected and most marginalized, in that dialogue, witness their livelihood and dignity being debated and discussed. If the only way that third way thinking works is by excluding those most affected, we should plainly say it doesn't work.

Involving only people who do not have an existential interest in the results of the dialogue is not a tenable solution, because ultimately it centers the powerful in the discussion and fails to listen to the most affected. The most affected need to be centered in a conversation and to have their voices elevated. We can see this in Acts 6, when the Greek-speaking Jews note to the Hebrew-speaking Jewish leadership that Greek-speaking Jewish widows are not getting the daily allotment of food. The leaders get together and call a group of people to address this issue. Here is how Luke puts it: "They chose Stephen, a man full of faith and the Holy Spirit, together with Philip, Prochorus, Nicanor, Timon, Parmenas, and Nicolaus, a proselyte of Antioch" (Acts 6:1–7). Why are those names significant? They're Greek names. When dealing with a material concern— such as the feeding of the widows—we can see it is essential to listen to and elevate the voices of those most affected.

I do believe that there is a time and place for third way thinking. I think it works best when the debate itself isn't existential and livelihood is not on the line. For example, there is a notable difference between finding a third way between pizza and tacos (perhaps by selecting burgers, because both parties also like burgers), and having a debate between whether or not we should be eating dinner at all. If the choice is between starving your family or feeding them, I do not think that finding a third way makes much sense. In the case of what's for dinner, everyone will ultimately be fed, so the stakes of the debate aren't as high. Certainly if someone were allergic to one of the foods in question, or perhaps a vegetarian, certain compromises and pathways would be immediately untenable.

There may be value in certain conflicts, where differences are mutual and not driven by power or social position, in pursuing a third way. But for many of the issues at hand that polarize our nation and our churches, a third way approach is not feasible, unless you intend to burden the most vulnerable with your compromise.

Notably, for our churches, we see the third way discussion occurring frequently when it comes to LGBTQIA inclusion. Seen as a political debate between holding on to traditional marriage and welcoming LGBTQIA people in marriage, ministry, and membership, many churches are at odds regarding how to satisfy both sides. But when the dignity of LGBTQIA people is on the line, any compromise is fundamentally dehumanizing to them. They are either fully dignified as individuals, or they are not. The suggestion that there is an in-between here perpetuates bigotry and increases harm.

The worst of this happens when a church offers a façade of inclusion and welcome, only to later inform LGBTQIA people that they can't serve in leadership, become a member, or get married. It is better to make your stance clear, instead of hiding it for the sake of a few extra people in attendance, or with the hope that you'll convert the LGBTQIA person to whatever ideology you espouse. That is a dangerous bait-and-switch and one worth rebuking.

I know this from personal experience. So while I could spend time dissecting third way statements of other churches, I want to acknowledge my own complicity in this and why this feels especially close to home to me. Circle of Hope, the cell church where I pastor, was not always a welcoming place for the LGBTQIA people. As a twenty-one-year-old cell leader, I knew this but still wanted to welcome everyone. I wanted my cell to multiply, I wanted to help recommend people to our covenant, I wanted to grow the church. I didn't know that by including them I was putting them in harm's way, but I admit that my lack of clarity and my naïveté did exactly that. For several months, I welcomed a few gay men into our cell. They were happy to participate, insightful, and longing for community and connection. But they bumped into the limits of our church when one of them shared on our public listserv that he had passed out fliers at Outfest, a festival for LBGTQIA folks to come out and be open about their gender and sexuality. The flier they passed out listed churches that were safe for LGBTQIA folks, and was distributed in response to a fundamentalist protest opposing the festival. Someone on our email listserv responded and asked if Circle of Hope was included on a website that listed welcoming churches, and if we should be. Our leadership was never clear about whether we should or shouldn't be listed based on our view of LBGTQIA inclusion; it was always a series of other excuses as to why we weren't. Our church heard from leaders of the church that email wasn't the right medium for this complex discussion; that we needed to have in-person conversations to address this nuanced and divisive matter. The truth is, our leaders were obfuscating the truth; in fact, I recall one of the leaders saying he was deliberately trying to confuse someone seeking a clear answer on LGBTQIA inclusion.

What followed was a series of email exchanges, public and private, as well as many meetings and phone calls. Up until this point Circle of Hope had prided itself on successfully avoiding a divisive issue, and we were content with having a "policy to not have a policy," or "a no-position position." The extent of our third way imaginative approach was simply to not have a position. The lack of clarity here was disingenuous because when it came to including LGBTQIA people, we had plain limitations. We wouldn't include LGBTQIA people in membership if they weren't celibate. So we were operating as what some have called side B, but because we weren't clear we could hardly have even claimed that status, which does provide a degree of safety for celibate LBGTQIA people. Here's how Justin Lee describes the differences between side A and side B: "In essence, Side A holds that gay sex (like straight sex) is morally acceptable in the right circumstances. Side B holds that gay sex is inherently morally wrong."[1] Side B Christians welcome LBGTQIA people so long as they are celibate.

At the time, Circle of Hope did not want to make its stance clear, but when the question was pushed, the dialogue changed. We heard all sorts of reasons for why we shouldn't be having this discussion. Some said it was inappropriate to have it over email. Others said it was divisive. And others even said that non-members shouldn't lead a discussion on the church's stance, especially when they regularly attend another church. To be sure, I was complicit as a volunteer leader in these discussions, and I parroted talking points early in my career that horrify me now. We lost members in the process, and the harm we caused, and I caused, was significant. Our third way approach had failed. We clearly weren't finding a creative path between poles, we had simply sided against LGBTQIA folks and refused to admit it.

Rumors around Circle of Hope's "no-position position" continued throughout the years. In 2013, though, three years after planting a church in North Philly, a reporter wrote a fairly positive piece on our church. In response to that positive article, some of the members of our church who were pushed out caught the story and decided to share their experience with Circle of Hope with the same reporter, who wrote another story that described their ousting. In that story, I avoided sharing many details, as I was instructed, and I told the reporter that our policy was to have no policy. The men in the story described me as toeing the party line even though they knew me to be "gay-affirming."[2] This created a lot of dialogue in our church, which was full of progressive Christians who were looking for an alternative to the Evangelical church.

The story broke at the end of November 2013, and by January 2014 we had changed policies. Faced with the harm we caused, and eager members ready to take a stand, we drafted a new statement on marriage that included a clause that allowed for faithful, long-term relationships between couples of the same sex. To be fair, we still tried to thread a needle, offering faithful options for inclusion for LBGTQIA folks who wanted to be celibate or who elected to remain in a straight marriage. As the years went on, we regularly updated our statement and our teachings to be more and more inclusive, including affirmation of transgender folks. We are now committed to listening to the voices of the most affected and submitting ourselves to their leadership.

It breaks my heart, to this day, to think of the harm I caused. I have reached out and tried to repent with those whom I hurt and I will continue to do so. This experience and the lived experience of LBGTQIA folks convicted me to take a stand, to stop trying to forge a third way when people's lives depended on it. No longer was this an issue that was between ideological poles—we were talking about human life and dignity. As I see Christians wrestle with taking a side, I encourage them to do so. We can—and must—be straightforward about what we believe. We don't need to take someone out to coffee and offer them a confusing response to a plainly worded question. If we feel shame about our beliefs, may that be a lesson for us that perhaps they are indeed shameful.

We can and should listen to the most affected instead of trying to forge a path over the top of them and their livelihoods. Equivocation when it comes to people's livelihoods can lead to loss of faith, loss of hope, even death. In fact, *religious* LGBTQIA people are more likely to be suicidal in large part because of direct condemnation or lack of commitment that third way churches offer.[3]

Churches then must take a stand, not a third way. For churches and people unable to take a moral stand for the sake of the lives and dignity of people, I believe one of the biggest growth edges is rooting our choices in people's real lives, not in reducing lives to mere ideological positions.

For Christians, we often hear of the need to put our identity in Christ above our worldly identities. Many Christian leaders teach that race is a social construct and sexuality is not an important part of who we are, and sometimes even a socially constructed part of who we are. Much of the meaning assigned to our body is indeed socially constructed, but that doesn't make it not a real part of who we are. Social constructions assign value, purvey real pain, and are inescapable to so many. Liberation looks like naming these categories and honoring them. Even if they do not have ontological weight—that is, exist as a part of our being—they are still part of our lived experience. So as long as we are on this side of heaven, we must consider them, even as we inaugurate a kingdom without such barriers.

In the age to come, I believe race, gender, sexuality, and ability will not divide us the way they do now. But I also believe the scars we have incurred because of them will stay with us, just like the scars of Jesus remained. Thomas feels Jesus' wounds in John 20:24–27. So these identities and experiences are not immaterial even if they are socially constructed. I want to avoid essentializing any of our identities as permanent, but I also want to honor them for how they have shaped us. I don't ever want to ask someone to discard their racial, gender, and sexual identities, because that would be asking them to discard parts of who they are—and Jesus asks us to bring our whole selves to him.

Christians frequently miss the mark when we ask one another to deny our humanity, to become less human, even, in order to cooperate and keep the peace in the church. Worse than that, we're asked to become less human to become more like God. If we don't, we're told that we are making our race, or gender, or sexuality a problem. Too often we think of existential matters as matters of philosophy. We turn our intractable poles into ones made of ideology, instead of ones on which people's humanity actually rests.

Our faith is about becoming more human, more in touch with who we truly are, through our intimacy with God and our relationship with Jesus. We celebrate the incarnation of Christ—Jesus becoming human—to become more human ourselves. In Christ, we become more fully who we are, and because of the abounding grace of God, we can enter fully into the pain we have experienced and the pain we have caused. We can enter fully into how the world has made us as we ask God to redeem it all. All of our experiences that have given our bodies political meaning can be redeemed through Christ and not discarded.

The committee that translated the Common English Bible translated the apocalyptic title for Christ, *ho huios tou anthropou* (ὁ υἱὸς τοῦ ἀνθρώπου), which New Testament writers borrow from Daniel 7:13 and is often translated as "Son of Man," as "the Human One." This term captures the fullness of the humanity of Christ—not just that he became human, but that in his incarnation he makes us more fully human, more fully who we are meant to be. Jesus makes us who we truly are by relating us to our creator personally, through his incarnation. The apostle Paul comments on this in his famous love chapter in 1 Corinthians:

> For now we see in a mirror, dimly, but then we will see face to face. Now I know only in part; then I will know fully, even as I have been fully known. (1 Corinthians 13:12)

As we relate to God we become more in touch with our own humanity and our collective humanity. The things that the world assigns meaning to in our bodies that oppress us are redeemed in Jesus. We don't need to distance ourselves from our lived experiences; we are permitted to enter into those experiences more fully. As we grow closer to God we become more fully ourselves—more substantive—and God gives new meaning to our bodies. I love how C.S. Lewis puts it in *The Great Divorce*, a novel he wrote about heaven and hell. When the narrator enters heaven, he remarks about how heaven's grass is more substantive than he is. It hurts him to walk on it:

> A grove of huge cedars to my right seemed attractive and I entered it. Walking proved difficult. The grass, hard as diamonds to my unsubstantial feet, made me feel as if I were walking on wrinkled rock, and I suffered pains like

those of the mermaid in Hans Andersen. A bird ran across in front of me and I envied it. It belonged to that country and was as real as the grass. It could bend the stalks and spatter itself with the dew.[4]

In this passage, even the grass—like all of heaven—is more real than the narrator. As we bring heaven to earth and grow closer to God, we are liberated from our oppression, and we live into our full humanity. Oppression makes us less real, less alive, less human—but following God is about becoming more human, as we become fully human in the age to come. Through Jesus' redemption, the pathway to our liberation is entering into the pain and suffering that we experience. Rather than distancing ourselves from our bodies to empathize with our oppressor, we can enter into our pain fully and make ourselves known. Christian politics and theology are never abstract; they are always embodied. We don't *have* a politics or a theology; we *are* a politics and a theology.

This embodied politics is an invitation for all of us to enter into the pain we have experienced and respond to it. We all can recall and reflect upon how we have been oppressed and see how that experience has shaped our politics. The binary between oppressed and oppressor is not always clear, and in our complex world, we are bound to have been oppressed in one way or the other. When we do this, we can empathize with the oppressed in a given circumstance, instead of using our experience as a way to combat the claims of the oppressed.

Too often we see our differences as purely ideological or philosophical, and as such unimportant or unessential. If we do not consider the material consequence of our politics, we may see stubborn, entrenched sides, and we may resist joining and rather attempt to transcend both of them. We may think that the debate about immigration is as inconsequential as one about pizza and tacos. For those who are not immigrants, it may seem as immaterial—but for those of us who are, it is far more dire.

We can see how the powerful, or those whom the status quo benefits, try to reduce bodily politics to mere ideology in how the term *woke* has gone from meaning racial awareness to a pejorative used against activism. The term *woke* has somewhat unclear origins, but in 1923 it appeared in the writings of Marcus Garvey, a Jamaican activist, when he implored his audience to "Wake up!" Then the term appeared again in Lead Belly's song entitled "Scottsboro Boys," written after the 1931 accusation of nine Black teens raping two White women in Scottsboro, Arkansas. At the conclusion of the song, he warns, "So I advise everybody, be a little careful when they go along through there—best stay woke, keep their eyes open." In both Lead Belly and Garvey's usage, being "woke" is about consciousness, and specifically Black consciousness. "Woke" means being aware of how to navigate the world as a Black individual. Black novelist William Melvin Kelley used the term in a piece he wrote for the *New York Times* in 1962. Commenting on the piece, writer Aja Romano said:

> Even in a piece largely focused on linguistics, Kelley directly connects "woke" Black culture back to an awareness of systematized white violence against Black people. Writing about the ephemeral nature of this shifting Black vernacular, he noted that many popular idioms among Black Americans have been loaded with coded precautions since the era of slavery.[5]

"Woke" is a part of African American vernacular meant to communicate consciousness to Black Americans, and to cloak its meaning from White Americans. To be woke means to be a conscious Black person navigating Whiteness. It grew in meaning and popularity during the start of the Black Lives Matter movement after the police killing of Michael Brown in Ferguson, Missouri. Because of the diversity of the movement, "woke" lost its exclusive Black meaning, but retained the idea surrounding Black consciousness and advocacy, this time lending itself to the movement for Black lives.[6]

As resistance to Black Lives Matter grew, so did resistance toward wokeness. In the summer of George Floyd's murder, conservative columnist David Brooks implied that wokeness was a "quasi-religion."[7] His colleague Bret Stephens likened it to the dystopian rule in Orwell's *1984,* calling it a game and an affront to "fairness" in the name of "claiming offense."[8] Yet another columnist from the same paper, Ross Douthat, simply referred to it in cosmopolitan terms, "the language of elite hyper-educated progressivism."[9] Rod Dreher called it "soft totalitarianism" and likened it to Bolshevism.[10]

What started as a matter of Black consciousness became derided as an ideology. Criticizing wokeness masks racism and anti-Blackness. Christian writer Danté Stewart names it plainly: "Let's be clear: the word 'woke' is just another word for Black. When people are talking about 'wokeness', they are talking about Black equality, Black dignity, and Black liberation. That is what they hate. They are anti-Black. It has always been about white supremacy and power."[11]

Stewart points out that when it comes to the politics of our body, we cannot sort through polarities as if they were merely ideologies. Criticizing wokeness too often means criticizing the Black bodies who are empowered and affirmed by such politics. In the case of LBGTQIA inclusion in churches, we are not simply discussing different theological viewpoints. When it comes to immigration, it's not just a matter of politics. When it comes to the lives of Black people, we aren't only debating social statements. A third way approach works when the stakes are low, when we're having a dialogue about abstract ideas, or when none of us are intimately affected by the ideas themselves. When the stakes are much higher for the most vulnerable, there is no third way—we either oppose the vulnerable or side with them.

Proponents of third way thinking insist that it is not moderation or a compromise between two positions, but a yet-to-be-imagined third possibility. In practice, though, those third way imaginations can seem to be ways to evade taking a stand. When it comes to the dignity of people's lives, I have yet to witness a third way approach that doesn't further oppression. Jesus doesn't offer a third way between oppressed and oppressor. Jesus sides with the oppressed.

Chapter 7

"Let Your Yes Be Yes"

We see over and over again that Jesus is not hesitant to make plain political commitments in order to advocate for and side with the oppressed. This sort of boldness is characteristic of Jesus, but it seems that advocates of the third way see Jesus as someone who is "politically homeless," and someone who forged a path between ideologies.

But throughout the Bible we see that Jesus actually encourages people to make political commitments. Rather than forging a third way, as some have suggested he does, he *deepens* the law and our commitment to it and radicalizes it further. The Sermon on the Mount, one of Jesus' main teachings in the gospel of Matthew, shows us how Jesus does this. For Anabaptists, the tradition I am a part of, the Sermon on the Mount is a central teaching in the Bible. In fact, in our church, we say we read the entire Bible from the Sermon on the Mount out. This teaching is often cited as a call to Christian creativity among intractable poles, but this decidedly worldly interpretation stems from the world's desire for a sort of apolitical reading of the gospel. The Sermon on the Mount is in fact deeply political and invested in moving followers of Jesus to make political commitments. It doesn't shy away from political commitments that necessarily place us on a side.

At the outset of Matthew 5, Jesus tells us who he is speaking to—who he chooses to speak to, who he is relating to, and who his ministry is for—when he lists the famous Beatitudes: the poor, the mournful, the meek, the hungry and thirsty, the merciful, the pure in heart, the peacemakers, and the persecuted—which is clearly demonstrated in Luke's telling of the Beatitudes (Luke 6). He says they will be reviled and persecuted; in other words, they will be oppressed. He names his oppressed audience as salt and light; the people who *season* the earth and bring out its flavor (just as salt does in its culinary applications). They are the light of the world. Jesus tells them that the city God is building, the kingdom God is inaugurating, is ushered in by these meek and lowly people to whom he is preaching.

Jesus then states the thesis of his sermon, which is to bring out the fullness of the law and apply it to a new context. Jesus is hardly eschewing the law and the religion of his fellow Jews—he is intensifying it. You might say he radicalizes it. In this Jesus is not forging another way, but deepening the way to follow him. The teachings of this Jesus, who is very interested in the material consequence of our faith, may feel like they do not square with the writings of the apostle Paul, who some read as de-emphasizing the law. But Paul de-emphasized the law insofar as it excluded Gentiles from fellowship. Jesus is intensifying the law as a matter of *righteousness* (Matthew 5:20), or *justice* as some translations put it. Jesus then goes on to tell us that anger and insults against our siblings make us liable to judgment, just as murder would. Jesus tells men that when they look upon a woman lustfully, it is as if they have committed adultery, and they should cut out their eyes or cut off their arms. He also radicalizes how we love, and commands us not to retaliate.

These are all clear political commitments. Jesus wants us to make our word true and wants the power of what we say to have substance. This is why he commands us not to take oaths, since our word is strong enough. But when we don't, when we obfuscate what we mean, when we try to play to both sides, when we don't make political commitments, our word becomes weak. Our yes cannot be a yes that is trustworthy (see Matthew 5).

In Matthew 7, at the conclusion of the Sermon on the Mount, Jesus tells us that he is not interested in people who are deceiving themselves as followers:

> Not everyone who says to me, "Lord, Lord," will enter the kingdom of heaven, but only the one who does the will of my Father in heaven. On that day many will say to me, "Lord, Lord, did we not prophesy in your name, and cast out demons in your name, and do many deeds of power in your name?" Then I will declare to them, "I never knew you; go away from me, you evildoers." (Matthew 7:21–23)

Jesus tells us that our confession in words is not enough. That we must follow the will of the Father. What we *do* matters as much as what we *say*, emphasizing that only those who do the will of the Father will enter into the kingdom. Jesus is concerned with actions as an indication of our being "pure in heart" (Matthew 5:8). The foundation of our faith is to act in a committed way, with resolve, according to the teachings of Jesus and the will of the Father.

Jesus' teaching in the Sermon on the Mount is not concerned with divisiveness, the appearance of being political, or navigating the world with nuance. It is an assertive message about deepening our commitments to a transformed life, one that places us on the side of the most vulnerable, the audience of the sermon itself, to inaugurate the kingdom of God. Jesus makes it plain that the condition of our heart will be made evident by the fruit of our labor. Our actions showcase what we are committed to. Jesus is asking us to let our yes be yes, to be trustworthy when we say we follow him.

A common critique of making plain and strong political commitments is born in Paul's word to the Corinthians:

> For though I am free with respect to all, I have made myself a servant[1] to all, so that I might win more of them. To the Jews I became as a Jew, in order to win Jews. To those under the law I became as one under the law (though I myself am not under the law) so that I might win those under the law. To those outside the law I became as one outside the law (though I am not free from God's law but am under Christ's law) so that I might win those outside the law. To the weak I became weak, so that I might win the weak. I have become all things to all people, that I might by all means save some. I do it all for the sake of the gospel, so that I may share in its blessings. (1 Corinthians 9:19–23)

Paul is demonstrating to the Corinthians how and why he chose to adapt himself to various ministerial contexts. He is demonstrating fidelity to culture and tradition when those things matter to advancing the gospel. He doesn't discard Jewish tradition when relating to Jews, those under the law. But when relating to people who weren't observing Jewish customs, those outside of the law, he doesn't observe those customs. In both cases, he names himself as not under the law but also beholden to Christ's law, so it is the law of Christ that moves him to be all things to all people. And to the weak, or to the oppressed in Corinth, the lowliest of people, Paul became like them, to win them over. He becomes all things to all people.

It's a beautiful vision of Christian humility and showcases the opportunity we all have to adapt and flex the gospel for contextual relevance. It shows us that we can change our evangelistic approach depending on the audience we face. And the New Testament is full of that kind of contextualization, which is why scholars and pastors like to understand the original context of the Bible—because audience and occasion are so important to understanding the meaning of the passage.

But Paul's humble approach, one he exemplifies in the epistles he writes to various churches across the Mediterranean, is often used to indict overtly political messages or commitments as inhospitable or not adapting to all people. Especially in politically pluralistic congregations, the most vulnerable are often told to cater their message to the skeptical. And the efficacy of their message and its messaging is judged based on how well it is received by the skeptical, who usually come from a position of power.

Failure to convince those in power of an urgent political or congregational issue, for example, becomes the burden of the oppressed. We are then made responsible for not being gentle enough, careful enough, or loving enough. These critics will tell us we aren't being all things to all people, or we aren't being Christlike enough. It is vulnerable minorities who, when making our own politics plain, or naming where we see and experience oppression, are told to make sure our words don't offend our audience. Oftentimes, we will hear something like, "I agree with everything you're saying, but not *how* you're saying it." But when so little advocacy on behalf of the oppressed is done by those who police their tone, it is hard to believe that to be true. *Tone policing* hits the oppressed while they're down, while ignoring their oppressor. It furthers oppression.

One of the issues here is that well-meaning people, who think of themselves as allies, who even consider themselves to be on the side of the oppressed, are the ones suggesting that vulnerable minorities change their tone. They usually think they have threaded the needle between oppressor and oppressed, and have an enlightened approach that is not of the world, but rather is of Jesus. They think they have found a third way. But they have not truly awakened to the oppression they are complicit in.

When the disciples of Jesus greet their liberator as he enters Jerusalem during the triumphal entry, the Pharisees tell Jesus to quiet them down—you might say "tone policing" them. Jesus says, "if these were silent, the stones would shout out" (Luke 19:39–40). The truth cannot be contained, and if it needs to be expressed in terms that are impolite, or even impolitic, that shouldn't stop us.

The problem here is the White moderate, as Martin Luther King named him in "The Letter from a Birmingham City Jail":

> I have been gravely disappointed with the white moderate. I have almost reached the regrettable conclusion that the Negro's great stumbling block in the stride toward freedom is not the White Citizens Councilor or the Ku Klux Klanner but the white moderate who is more devoted to order than to justice; who prefers a negative peace which is the absence of tension to a positive peace which is the presence of justice; who constantly says, "I agree with you in the goal you seek, but I can't agree with your methods of direct action."[2]

King is naming the issue with "tone policing" oppressed minorities, instead of confronting their oppressor. In a more intimate setting, you'll hear the White moderate offer the benefit of the doubt to the individual who is causing harm to the vulnerable when they claim (or feign) ignorance. At that point, the oppressed person is then asked to make sure the message is spoken in a way that helps them be heard by their oppressor. In other words, the oppressed person becomes responsible for their own oppression because they did not treat their oppressor with the right tone. They weren't "all things to all people." And to claim that that is what being all things to all people is adds spiritual abuse to this emotional abuse.

We see this today in the critical reaction to the protests against police brutality in 2020. One moderate columnist joined right-wing commentators in suggesting that the increase in homicides in major cities in the United States was linked to a "demoralized police force." He argued that unless the language of the activists changed, Trump could be reelected in 2024. He also argued that unless Biden laid out a strong anti-crime plan, one that supported the police (instead of dismantling them), Trump could be reelected. The columnist went on to quote a story in the *Star Tribune* of Minneapolis that cites only police department officials as suggesting a causal connection between the rise in Minneapolis homicides and the protests: "Department officials say it is no coincidence that the rise in crime comes after the departure of at least 200 members of the city's police force ."[3] But the labor data actually suggests something much different. In 2020, when the United States lost six percent of its labor force, police departments lost just one percent of their labor force.[4] Here the columnist is blaming minorities for their own oppression because of the rhetoric they employed in response to George Floyd's murder.

Well-meaning White people tone police minorities because it is easier for them to name a strategic problem than it is to confront racism or any kind of prejudice on its head. Support for Black Lives Matter peaked in June 2020 among White people, but has been on a steady decline ever since then. In fact, in September 2020 it was down 12 percentage points across all demographics, with White folks leading the decline by 15 percentage points (meanwhile, Black support *grew* over that period).[5] By April 2021, White support declined even further, with Black support, and support among all racial minorities, remaining stable. The support of White folks was "both fickle and volatile."[6] What we're seeing here isn't that the messaging was weak, it's that White support for the movement for Black lives is. That's because we are battling something much more than just the right or wrong tone—we are battling the force of racism. And these examples show us that King's warning against White moderates is a continuing problem.

The demands of the tone police are not in line with Paul's vision in 1 Corinthians 9. The idea that the oppressed person should meet their oppressor where they are is not what Paul is modeling. Paul, as we know from his letters, is someone who is in a position of power both in the Jewish community and in Rome. In Acts 22:28, Luke quotes Paul as naming himself born a Roman citizen after he is arrested. His Roman citizenship spares his life. Some people say Paul is invoking his power and privilege here. But in doing this he simply acnkowledges that he comes from a position of power, and it is through this light we should read his teachings, which consistently signal a desire to divest that power. In Philippians 3:5–6 Paul describes himself as the model Jew, having been "circumcised on the eighth day, a member of the people of Israel, of the tribe of Benjamin, a Hebrew born of Hebrews; as to the law, a Pharisee; as to zeal, a persecutor of the church; as to righteousness under the law, blameless." Because he's a Jew, he can meet the Jews where they are. Because he has a Roman background and feels free from the law, he can do the same. But when he gets to describing the weak, whom he sees as the oppressed, he becomes oppressed himself.

Paul's method for ministering to the oppressed is to put himself in their position. This is why in 2 Corinthians 11 and 12, he boasts in his weakness—it is not through earthly power that he is saved, but through grace alone, where God's power is made perfect in weakness. Christians are then free to divest their power because in their weakness and in their oppression, God's power is magnified. To be sure, this is a message Paul is delivering to those with a lot of earthly power, like the wealthy members of the socially stratified Corinthian community.

In 2 Corinthians 5, he shows us the vision of the new humanity, the new creation, he is helping to bring to life in Corinth. He says that "we regard no one from a human point of view" (5:16). And through this vision for a new creation, one where we have all divested our power, we join God in the "ministry of reconciliation," or better put, "the ministry of justice"—the ministry of making the wrongs of the world right, the ministry that expresses the atonement of Jesus on the cross, the great rectification and restitution, in our daily lives in our worshiping communities.

In Romans 6, Paul says that we are no longer bound to the way of the world, the way of sin. We are no longer servants of sin, expressed in the oppressive, death-making systems of this world, but rather we are servants of dikaiōsis (δικαίωσις), servants of justice. Paul's vision for the church is one where power is divested so that we can freely meet everyone where they are. Paul can be a Greek to the Greeks because he is not committed to his status in the Jewish community. He can be a Jew to Jews because he is ready to forfeit his Roman citizenship for that. And he can be the weak to the weak because he has chosen to let go of his worldly power for the sake of discipleship. In 1 Corinthians 9, Paul is asking us to demonstrate the humility to meet the oppressed where they are at; he is certainly *not* asking the weak to meet the strong where they are at, because that would further oppression. That request would simply be conforming to the patterns of this world (to borrow another Pauline phrase, this time from Romans 12) because it is the exact circumstance that the oppressed are in.

Faced with the challenge of moving people who are accustomed to their power to release that power, minorities are often burdened with the responsibility to perfectly message their viewpoint to accommodate the powerful and hope they change. We are asked to debase ourselves just for the opportunity to be heard, as if all that is missing from our messages is politeness. And when we fail to be seen, the burden is placed on us again: the fault is ours for not being gentle enough, dialogical enough, or open enough. Rarely does that burden fall on the self-proclaimed ignorant person, who naïvely wields their power in a way that furthers oppression. That is far beyond the vision for the community that Paul lays out in his letters. Paul is asking the powerful to become servants of justice in order to become weak to meet the weak.

The posture of our communities then needs to be one that serves the oppressed and meets them where they are, instead of expecting them to meet their oppressors that way. Within that framework, though, there is room for diversity of messaging. We should cater our message to the people in front of us, but we can never allow it to come at the expense of the most vulnerable. The burden must always fall with the powerful, with the strong.

There are times to mind our messaging, but in politically pluralistic congregations or in racially diverse conversations, it is impossible and inadvisable to appeal to everyone at the same time and expect to have strong messaging that advocates for the oppressed. Put another way, it is impossible to appeal to everyone without burdening the oppressed more. Ultimately we have to make our yes a yes and decide who we will burden more: the oppressed or the oppressor. Even through this, Jesus transforms us beyond these binaries. In fact, a biblical hermeneutic that favors the oppressed and explores how we are all often oppressed in one way or another can bring a diverse group together.

We do have different ministerial contexts; we live in different geographical and socioeconomic areas; the politics of our surrounding regions may differ. Because of this, we can expect that messaging around how we live out Paul's vision to become servants of righteousness—those who do the will of the Father, as Jesus puts it—to be different. There are entire fields of theology that specialize in the contextualization to offer the gospel to all people by all means. There are contextual theologies that focus, for example, on Black women, or Latina women, or disabled people, or other groups of marginalized people, which mainstream (read: White, male) theology has excluded. Embracing Paul's vision means not trying to speak to everyone at the same time but focusing on the groups that are marginalized and oppressed. We become weak for the sake of the weak, and by all means.

It makes sense to cater our messages to move our people along with the vision of God. This becomes more challenging when we have diverse communities, but embracing the lived experience of those vulnerable people we are fortunate enough to include in our communities helps move these conversations from abstract to material. So we should not rest on our laurels if our communities are conveniently monolithic; we should preference the oppressed in our communities—and our communities, no matter where we live, have oppressed people who are possibly being displaced by our preference to accommodate the oppressor. We should keep trying to convince the skeptical, but not at the expense of the marginalized.

The best way to do this is to elevate the stories of the oppressed, and their voices; to listen to them and what they say; to allow them to challenge your way of doing things, even when it's uncomfortable. Leaders may be fearful to do this since we may lose participants in our church, but what good is it to gain the whole world, yet forfeit your soul? Faithfulness matters more than success. Further, Jesus promised us we would incur a loss as a result of following him. But we shouldn't fear, because we can trust that there are people around our communities who are moved by the Holy Spirit and will join us. We should not be looking to change everyone's minds, but rather to find the people who have softened hearts and are ready to follow Jesus radically. If we focus on our most hostile people and try to accommodate them, we are doomed to fail to convince them, and also to comfort and aid those they afflict and oppress.

We need not shy away from political commitments, but rather must make them boldly, for the sake of the oppressed and the most vulnerable. We do this to meet the weak, the lowly, and the oppressed where they are so that we can help inaugurate this radical kingdom of God, this new humanity, this new creation, where the ways of the world are turned upside down.

Chapter 8

The Kingdom of God Is Not Bipartisan

"In politics, the Middle Way is none at all."
—John Adams

Bipartisanship—cooperation across difference, being able to accomplish things despite political diversity—is an important part of American mythology. Americans idealize uniting together to work toward a common end. We see it as productive, decent, and mature. Christians are no strangers to the allure of bipartisanship, either. Many pastors who try to appear nonpartisan name Jesus as being neither liberal nor conservative. They rebuke people who make their politics plain, saying that it demonizes the other side. Those who espouse the third way talk down to people who are serious about the threats of creeping fascism, nationalism, and White supremacy. You hear them name progressives and conservatives as two sides of the same coin, claiming partisanship is the evil, instead of the content of the politics themselves. Here's how one pastor, who prides himself on apoliticality and borrows some of his thinking from Anabaptists, put it:

> After two National Conventions we have FINALLY found
> a conviction both sides can passionately agree on: America
> will enter the apocalypse if the opposing side wins! If we do
> not outgrow this venomous "You-Are-An-Enemy" mind-
> set, both sides will eventually be proven right.[1]

I was astonished by this tweet from a White cisgender
male pastor, since White supremacy, in the 2020 presidential election, was on the ballot. And today, White supremacy
remains a viable political option for many, and apparently, to
those unaffected by it, one that shouldn't be resolutely condemned. For people of color, though, people who hate them
are indeed enemies, and the revealing of White supremacy
does truly feel apocalyptic. According to the pastor quoted
above, the real problem is hostility between parties. For people of color, though, the major issue is racialized harm and
abuse that can come from the Republican party, including,
for example, the zero-tolerance immigration policy of the
Trump administration.

What we hear is that resistance to polarity and partisanship
is a new or different approach to politics. But it is just more of
the same. Bipartisanship, cooperation, and shared interests are
not an alternative to the American way of doing things; they
are emblematic of America. Trying to strike a balance between
political poles, or finding a moderate path between them, isn't
a radical alternative, it's exactly what the story of the United
States and its way of governance is laid on. National unity
with shared interests is fundamentally a part of the American
project. National unity without reckoning for the oppressed
burdens them more than anyone. National unity without
radical reform keeps things running as they are. It is through
strong partisanship that change can happen. Unfortunately,
partisanship and sidedness are nearly universally decried as

negative, especially by our leaders. The pastor above may have thought he was resisting the cultural narrative, but in fact, he was reiterating it.

We see the same thing when politicians proclaim values of both justice and bringing a polarized community together—inevitably, one must fall when one side stands in the way of justice. For example, Joe Biden ran his presidential campaign on bringing a polarized nation together while naming the dangers of the hatred that was being stoked. Biden's focus to unite the country, without dealing with what is dividing us, is naïve. His answers are "tolerance and humility," being "willing to stand in the other person's shoes just for a moment." This pie-in-the-sky characterization of what will overcome our fierce divisions that date back to Lincoln's Emancipation Proclamation may be appropriate for an inaugural address, but it rings hollow to the people who are impacted most by that division. When Biden says to unite despite our differences, he's asking me to put aside my humanity. When he asks me to put myself in someone else's shoes, I am putting myself in the shoes of someone who hates me. What divides us in the United States, and what prevents bipartisanship, is much deeper than a conflict between two families or two tribes.

Biden's idealism about unity and bipartisanship has foiled his agenda, however. He campaigned on unity and bipartisanship, but those were not the tools he needed to advance the causes he campaigned for. In fact, Biden's flagship legislation, the Build Back Better bill, died because of the filibuster rule and Joe Manchin's lack of support.[2] After this, Biden's effort to pass voting rights legislation similarly failed, once again at the hands of Manchin, Kyrsten Sinema, and the Senate's outdated rules.[3]

Consensus-driven governments and decisions often uphold the worst parts of society, and while they are praised for how they appear, they simply maintain the status quo. They can hide corruption underneath the guise of peace. James Madison argued that bipartisanship risks tyrannical reins of power, which is ironic since proponents of bipartisanship and the filibuster argue tyranny will follow if we become led by a single party. In Federalist Paper No. 10, Madison argued that partisanship and sharp debates between parties actually lead to a free society. Not only did bipartisanship protect slavery, it "allowed racial segregation after the Civil War and the internment of Japanese-Americans during WWII."[4] It made McCarthyism possible. And in 2002, the quagmire war in Iraq enjoyed bipartisan support. Whereas partisanship, which is often used as a pejorative, created the Bill of Rights, ended slavery, created trust-busting laws, and is why we have Social Security now.[5] Bipartisanship is an impediment to progress, and partisanship, in fact, is what is needed to make real change that positively impacts the lives of the oppressed.

When it comes to politics that affect the lives of the oppressed, a bipartisan approach often functionally works to hollow out laws that purport to bring positive reform and change, while also maintaining the optics of cooperation and unity. Christian advocates of the third way, who define it as a middle road, or making sure we listen to both sides or even hold both sides together, are not demonstrating a Christian alternative, but rather, simply maintaining the status quo.

When we as Christians proclaim moderation as a radical alternative to the political, sided, and partisan way of the world, we are actually doing quite the opposite. The way of the world is based on mutual interests that maintain the status quo. The way of Jesus challenges the ways of the world and doesn't seek a path of moderation between them. Jesus risked his popularity and his image for the least of these. He was accused of associating with sinners and tax collectors by the religious rulers of the day (Mark 2:13–17). When he faced the ruling political and religious parties of his time, the Pharisees and the Sadducees, he didn't moderate between them; in fact, as we saw in the Sermon on the Mount, he radicalized the teaching of the Pharisees, with whom he spent a lot of time.

Though the Pharisees and the Sadducees were the main sects of Judaism during the time of Jesus, as Josephus, the Roman-Jewish historian, shows us,[6] there were two other sects as well. The Essenes were a separatist sect that largely did not live in Jerusalem. They were similar to the Pharisees, but even more radically separatist, and were probably from the Qumran community, which is credited with writing the Dead Sea Scrolls. The other group, what Josephus calls the "fourth sect," scholars understand as the Zealots, who had an "inviolable attachment to liberty; and say that God is to be their only Ruler and Lord."[7]

The truth is we do not know a lot about these sects conclusively, and for our purposes, the Pharisees specifically. Most of what we know comes from Josephus, Jewish literature, and the New Testament. Too often scholars romanticize the Pharisees or conclude too certainly about them, even when the hypotheses they offer are highly speculative.[8] As I discuss them, I will largely use what we know from the Gospels and how they related to Jesus.

Jesus' relationship with the Pharisees was complicated; at times, he was critical, other times he honored them, and still other times he related intimately with them (see John 3, when Jesus related to Nicodemus). The gospel of Luke shows the Pharisees as people Jesus respected, ate with, and related to. In Luke 11, Jesus shared their concern for ritual purity, but he radicalized it, demonstrating what the Pharisees already know: that cleanliness is a matter of both internal and external action. Jesus never condemned the Pharisees for their fidelity to the law, but rather condemned them for their hypocrisy. He names them as holding on to minor matters of the law but neglecting the major ones. He never dismissed their concern, but added to it. Jesus' fulfillment of the law (Matthew 5:17) showcased his own alignment with the Pharisees, whom he saw as siblings. Jesus joined the Pharisees in their opposition to the Sadducees.[9] [10] Between the two ruling parties, Jesus was most closely connected to the Pharisees, radicalizing their teaching, instead of forging a moderate position between the two.

The Sadducees were the ruling party during Jesus' lifetime, composed of wealthy and educated Jews who assimilated to life in Rome, making them the most Hellenized of the Jewish sects. The Sadducees focused on temple worship, believed in free will, didn't believe in the resurrection of the dead, and thought that God was removed from everyday affairs.[11] Jesus and the Pharisees clashed with them regularly, and the Gospels portray them as the primary enemy of Jesus. Annas and Caiaphas, the two high priests who colluded with Rome to kill Jesus, were Sadducees themselves.

Jesus didn't find a peaceable path between the Pharisees and the Sadducees. When the Pharisees warned Jesus that Herod was trying to kill him, Jesus named himself as a prophet, one who speaks the truth to power, unafraid of the consequences that may follow. His retort to the Pharisees after they warned him was incisive:

> Jerusalem, Jerusalem, the city that kills the prophets and stones those who are sent to it! How often have I desired to gather your children together as a hen gathers her brood under her wings, and you were not willing! See, your house is left to you. And I tell you, you will not see me

until the time comes when you say, "Blessed is the one who comes in the name of the Lord." (Luke 13:34–35)

Jesus disrupted the norms of his day to the point of death. Jesus channeled the spirit of the prophets of old, ready to be confronted by the ruling powers when he disrupted them. Just like it is unpopular to be evidently partisan, Jesus embraced the lack of popularity of his decided positions. He named Herod as a fox, and taunted him, as he continued to do his work of healing, driving out our demons. He kept pressing on despite the threats from the powers. He wasn't finding a bipartisan solution that offended no one, but for the sake of the least of these, Jesus pressed forward regardless of how the rulers scoffed at him. He was like Elijah when he confronted King Ahab, whose foreign wife, Jezebel, worshiped another god. Ahab had led Israel to dishonor God by associating with worshippers of Baal. It's the same sort of sinful assimilation that the Sadducees were engaged in with Rome, which named Caesar as Lord. When Elijah confronted Ahab, Ahab called him a "troubler of Israel" (1 Kings 18:17). Elijah embraced the "good trouble" that he was getting into (to quote the late John Lewis) and he confronted King Ahab for worshiping Baal and offending God. He then showcased Yahweh's power over Baal and humiliated the prophets of Baal and Ahab.

This prophetic tradition of making a clear, and perhaps partisan, stance against evil and for the oppressed is not of the world. In fact, a fake peace that is not real peace is what is popular. Unity without transformation maintains the status quo. That is the fruit of our insistence on bipartisanship as a way to lead and govern. Christians should be extremely partisan as we take the side of the least of these and avoid the temptation to silence our prophetic voices for the sake of appearing peaceful. No, in fact—to make peace, we must make our political commitments clear.

Does this mean we are doomed to be divided as a church or as a country? No. Unity is possible, but what unifies is the lordship of Jesus who serves the oppressed and makes his sidedness clear. Without transformation or repentance, those who oppress us cannot be united with us. True unity is a call for the oppressors to repent; they are welcome to join the movement, but they will have to lay down their power and move with the God of the oppressed. Bipartisanship with a hostile, obstructionist party is useless if it deprives the least among us of their basic dignity. The spirit of bipartisanship is purposed to keep things as they are, and its proponents advocate for it for those reasons.

But the church must lead differently, with nerve, for the sake of Christ and for the oppressed. This means we move forward, despite appearances of partisanship, for the sake of the oppressed. Undeterred by being named as partisan, we welcome the critique, because being partisan on behalf of the oppressed is exactly what Jesus does. Being united while stepping on the oppressed is not to be lauded, but rather condemned.

Karl Barth, the Swiss reformed theologian, says it clearly:

> God stands at every time unconditionally and passionately on this and only on this side: always against the exalted and for the lowly, always against those who already have rights and for those from whom they are robbed and taken away. [12]

Jesus isn't forging a moderate path between oppressed and oppressor. He is siding with the least of these; he's making a partisan stance. Following his lead, we must do the same, despite what our rulers ask of us.

Chapter 9

The Love of Christ Constrains Us to Vote

One of the most practical ways to take a side, and to make political commitments, is to vote. People having access to vote easily allows change to happen and people's voices to be heard. Voting is serious and it takes sober reflection to discern how, when, and if to vote. In this chapter, my goal is to showcase the importance of voting and offer us two circumstances where I felt moved to vote and where I felt unable to vote.

I believe Christians need to make political commitments to advocate for voting rights, which may be a curious position to take as an Anabaptist, because we historically have been engaged in nonresistance, which would include not voting. In Anabaptist circles, nonresistance refers to not physically or violently resisting any authority, even if it is evil. But nonresistance met some limitations during the civil rights movement in the United States thanks to the work of Vincent and Rosemarie Harding, two Black Mennonite leaders in Atlanta who tried to help a peace community engage in the freedom movement. Their commitment to Anabaptism and their lived experience as Black people in the South during the civil rights movement led them to

challenge this commitment to nonresistance. With the support
of the Peace Section of Mennonite Central Committee (MCC),
the Hardings formed Mennonite House, which helped MCC
think more critically and creatively about how it might engage
with the freedom movement. The house was opened with
"the explicit purpose of establishing a Mennonite presence in
the Freedom Movement and connecting Mennonite volunteers
with the work of the Movement." Because of this work, the
Peace Section acknowledged the limitations of nonresistance,
stating, "Christian obedience may at times lead to violation
of government laws and regulations." The lived experience of
the Hardings led to challenging the idea of nonresistance and
encouraged White Mennonites and Anabaptists to take action
to ally with their oppressed Black and Brown siblings.[1]

The results of our political processes are too dire to simply allow nonresistance, alone, to guide us. Voting can be an
expression of our fidelity to Christ when we embrace it as an
opportunity to join with him in advocating for the oppressed
and bringing about a more just nation and society, and we
should see this right and opportunity as a *practical* expression, not a *moral* one. This distinction is important because
the more we name voting as holy, as moral, as righteous even,
we tie our hands as Christians—as participants in an imperfect
system in an imperfect world, we will invariably compromise
our morality or our holiness or our righteousness when we
vote for a less-than-perfect leader. If we make it a moral choice,
we may elect not to vote at all, so that we might stay "pure."
However, because voting itself is not a matter of purity, neither
is non-voting. We don't escape participating in the system by
simply abstaining from voting.

When we make voting a moral imperative, we turn a practical matter of choosing the lesser of two evils into a matter

of faithfulness. This makes the stakes of voting too high, and may leave many of us unable to vote at all. Too often, we place an incredible responsibility on ourselves to right the wrongs of the world with our vote. We feel like we need to agree with everything a candidate stands for to make an ethical choice to vote for them. But for me, I'm selecting the best of the options before me, instead of making a moral endorsement of one of them. We are free in Christ to make choices without condemnation. This liberates us to vote without fear of electing a person who will be engaged in some harm, because we are not responsible, ultimately, for all of the decisions our leaders make. Rather, we exercise influence over what we can.

The freedom I feel to vote for an imperfect candidate, the better of the two evils, comes from Paul's vision of Christian freedom:

> For you were called to freedom, brothers and sisters; only do not use your freedom as an opportunity for self-indulgence, but through love become slaves to one another. For the whole law is summed up in a single commandment, "You shall love your neighbor as yourself." (Galatians 5:13–14).

Paul tells us explicitly how we are to use this freedom—not for "selfish impulses," but to serve one another, and to love one another as ourselves. This framework gives us freedom to act without fear of becoming impure, and the onus to act for the sake of loving our neighbor. How then does a Christian vote? Too often, Christians vote for the state to protect their interests, their liberties, their rights. Yet if the state ends up protecting the church and its freedoms and its right to exist, the church becomes an agent of the state. We can expect the world to hate us if we serve Christ, so rather than protecting ourselves, we must vote for the least of these, and with our neighbors in mind.

There may be times when we might elect not to vote at all. I reserve the right not to do so if the choices the parties have given me are inadequate. And in 2020, that almost became the case. As I will showcase later in this chapter, it was paramount to remove Donald Trump from office in that election cycle. For many, the language that surrounded Trump's removal was desperate. "Vote blue, no matter who" was the slogan. In a sense, this slogan discouraged the typical competition of the Democratic primary in 2020 for fear that party infighting might propel Donald Trump to another victory. But when Michael Bloomberg entered the race, I wondered if I could be compelled to vote between two billionaires and what it meant for the United States that candidates could simply buy themselves into the election.

Bloomberg's record on race relations was pitiful, and not a far cry from Donald Trump's own. Bloomberg defended "stop and frisk," also known as Terry stop, as a way to curb crime. The term comes from the 1968 U.S. Supreme Court case that argued police could search suspects and civilians with only "reasonable suspicion" instead of "probable cause." The court ruled that those stops do not violate the U.S. Constitution's opposition to unreasonable search and seizure. Practically that means police can search anyone they are reasonably suspicious of as long as they have enough "articulable facts"—which simply means that they can specifically describe their suspicion. The hurdle needed to clear reasonable suspicion with articulable facts is lower than what is needed for probable cause, and thus, use of the former are more common.[2]

This policy quickly became racialized in New York City, as well other cities. Bloomberg once noted he had a preference for more Terry stops in Black and Brown neighborhoods because he thought police were stopping "whites too much and minorities too little."[3] Black and Brown people were stopped in New York City 87 percent of the time in 2011, and there were more instances of stops of young Black men than there *were* young Black men in that same time period. Not only is the policy racist, it's also ineffective—it has a 90 percent failure rate. And crime actually dropped in 2013 when Terry stops also dropped.[4]

I wrote a blog post about not needing to vote when Bloomberg splashed onto the Democratic primary scene. When I shared it, many people were concerned that I was empowering the indifferent, fueling the idea that both sides were as bad as one another. In fact, they thought I might be the kind of person I wrote this book to critique! People told me that not voting came from a place of privilege, a place where politics were abstract, and that this isn't a position that minorities oppressed by Donald Trump could be in.

The issue with a principled stance to *not vote* is the same as a principled stance *to vote*. In general, voting is worth the amount of time it takes to do it. Giving it more power than that, whether you vote or don't, becomes its own form of idolatry. Not being willing to vote for anyone who compromises any of our beliefs would render us unable to participate at all. But participating in humility, in collaboration, on coalitions, is part of engaging in politics, and perhaps even expressive of Christian charity. Simply not participating, and not doing our earnest part to prevent a tyrant from remaining in office, is the same sort of indifference that Pontius Pilate displayed. Pilate tried to wash his hands of the execution of Jesus when he learned that opposing the crowd would lead to a decrease in his popularity, and he was in a politically precarious position. Pilate's decision not to participate did not make him any less complicit in the death of Jesus. From Matthew's gospel:

So when Pilate saw that he could do nothing, but rather that a riot was beginning, he took some water and washed his hands before the crowd, saying, "I am innocent of this man's blood; see to it yourselves." Then the people as a whole answered, "His blood be on us and on our children!" So he released Barabbas for them; and after flogging Jesus, he handed him over to be crucified. (Matthew 27:24–26)

Pilate tried to wash his hands of his indifference, of his lack of courage, but he couldn't. Just like we do, he bore the responsibility for his action and his inaction. Not participating doesn't make us any purer than participating does. Our choice to vote, then, is not a matter of moral purity or ideological consistency, but simply a practical matter. In most cases, it is worth taking a stand.

In 2020, I made the strongest appeal I've ever made to vote against Donald Trump, and I did so with much trepidation, not because it wasn't manifestly clear what a danger Donald Trump was, but because voting for Joe Biden, considering his record, was a complicated suggestion.

But despite Biden's problems, my love of neighbor, my advocacy for the least among us, moved me to vote for Biden in order to oppose Trump. This was not a radical statement, as many leaders, even Evangelical leaders who would normally back the Republican candidate, said similar things. For me, it was a unique expression because of my general posture toward voting as a practical and not a moral matter. Somehow, Trump was so wicked, that the line between the practical and the moral blurred, and I felt, *for the first time in my life*, morally compelled to vote, in order to vote against him.

Our commitment to advocating for the oppressed can inform not only our choice to vote, but to advocate for policies that make it as easy as possible for people to vote—as we see laws target the voting rights of people on the margins by making it more difficult for them to vote or diminishing the impact of their vote. This could include granting days off on Election Day, allowing for mail-in voting at every election, offering on-site registration, ending voter-ID laws, and also prohibiting gerrymandering, a practice that draws up voting districts with partisan interest in mind. The freedom to vote is actually an issue we *can* vote on because these laws are bound up in the state legislatures and Congress, right now. In fact, the result of the 2022 midterm elections themselves may offer us a pathway to increase the enfranchisement of the oppressed among us.

Another way to improve our electoral system on behalf of the oppressed is through ranked-choice, or scored-choice voting, instead of single voting or plurality voting. Single voting and plurality voting often reward the extreme candidates, as people's votes for moderate choices often dilute support for more moderate choices. To give you an example, if we are using single or plurality voting for electing the best pizza toppings, a small plurality supporting pineapple could defeat a majority of people opposing pineapple, by diluting their votes on sausage, pepperoni, and plain pizza. Even if the sausage, pepperoni, and plain pizza voters would all agree to one of the other options instead of pineapple, if the plurality wins, then pineapple wins. But if we ranked or scored our voting, we might end up ordering a pizza that most people like enough to eat, and not have to suffer from pineapple extremism.

For a live example, let's briefly look at the Democratic primary of 2020. Bernie Sanders, the democratic socialist from Vermont, won the Democratic primaries in Iowa, New Hampshire, and Nevada. In order to defeat him, the moderate candidates all stepped down and endorsed Biden, making it a two-way race between Biden and Sanders. If ranked-choice were an option, we may not have ended up with a race between the most progressive and most moderate candidate (or let's say the most "established" candidate), and perhaps a more progressive choice would even have emerged victorious. For radicals reading this, ranked-choice voting may seem like a negative thing, but ultimately, it is a more cohesive way to vote, as it doesn't allow extremist candidates to win. Along with the aforementioned ease in voting, we are not necessarily doomed to moderate results with ranked-choice voting, either.

It is the love of Christ that must constrain us or compel us to vote. Using our vote to benefit the downtrodden, the ones without rights, the ones who cannot be represented, is what moves us to exercise this democratic right. This includes children, immigrants, the elderly, and people with disabilities, who face obstacles to voting as well. It is the love of Christ that compels us to engage in what Paul calls the "ministry of reconciliation" or the ministry of justice. We advance the cause of justice when we vote in the interest of the least of these, and not ourselves. We vote to lower hills, and fill valleys, to uplift the weak, and bring down the powerful. We vote in alliance with Jesus, who is in the least among us.

Chapter 10

A Politically Prophetic Imagination

As Christians, we act politically in the present moment to do what we can now for marginalized and oppressed people. But we do not do so because it brings about the age to come or the fullness of our salvation. We act politically because we are motivated by the conviction of the Spirit, but our hope as Christians ultimately lies elsewhere. The Son of Man did not come to bring about a new political apparatus, he came to inaugurate a new kingdom, to reveal a new way of doing things, a new consciousness. He did that in the Spirit of the prophets of old.

Without a doubt, the lordship of Jesus is fundamentally a political act. That political act does help us to act immediately in our political economies, but it also motivates us to imagine a world beyond our political parameters. Too often radical ideas that emerge from the Bible, from the Spirit, from the saints, are tamped down as unrealistic or impractical considering our contemporary political restraints. The political systems in our world are designed to be self-perpetuating, so they naturally do not have mechanisms that challenge them.

This is where "prophetic imagination" comes in. Walter Brueggemann uses this term in a book with the same title. He writes, "The task of prophetic imagination is to cut through the numbness, to penetrate the self-deception so that the God of endings is confessed as Lord."[1] Brueggemann reminds us that "Jesus is Lord" is indeed a political statement. The lordship of Christ is so *real*, in fact, that living in any other way, what he terms the "royal consciousness," isn't actual reality—it is in fact, deception.

For Brueggemann, the prophetic imagination, first imagined by God through Moses and then through Jesus, creates "countercommunity with a counterconsciousness." Brueggemann suggests that countercommunity's goal is demonstration, not activism or social action. Moses was not engaged in regime change, but rather sought to critique "the consciousness that undergirded and made such a regime possible." This moves us to a more radical sort of political engagement, one that doesn't seek "betterment through the repentance of the regime," but rather a total undoing of the order for a "new reality to appear."[2] Brueggemann writes, "The alternative consciousness to be nurtured, on the one hand, serves to criticize in dismantling the dominant consciousness."[3]

Brueggemann acknowledges that the counterconsciousness of Moses was unlikely to sustain a religious, sociopolitical order for long. He also notes that justice and compassion are elemental to God's consciousness, but are so rarely prominent features of any historical community.[4] He does not shy away from naming that the transcendence of God is a direct affront to the highest powers. This is good news to "marginal people if they are to have a legitimate standing ground against" oppressors, but it is decidedly not what those "who regulate and benefit from the order of the day" want.[5]

Brueggemann clearly aligns God with the oppressed and purposes the prophetic imagination as a way to criticize and dismantle the dominators, while also demonstrating a new way of living and being, with God's freedom, justice, and compassion guiding its politics.[6] Brueggemann is certainly not advocating for political quietism, but rather a politics so radical that it upends how the entire world works; it is a politics from God that aligns with the oppressed, and it is with prophetic imagination that we engage in politics now.

In Jesus's birth, life, and resurrection we find both a deep criticism of the current cultural consciousness and also a demonstration of a new way of being, Brueggemann argues. In his birth, Jesus confronts Herod and lifts up the shepherds, a lowly class of people.[7] His acts of compassion critique the powers' indifference to the pain and suffering of the marginal. Even in his death, Jesus is not merely making a sacrifice, he is confronting the power of death itself. [8]

Not only does Jesus critique the powers, but he also showcases an entirely other way of doing things. The angels greet the birthed Lord with a new song; Mary sings, as opposed to making a decree, about God's fulfilled promises. In his ministry Jesus demonstrates a new consciousness as he relates to the marginalized and the outcast. The same is true for his radical teachings, which Brueggemann describes as "shattering and inviting." And finally, in his resurrection, Jesus displaces the old king, Death, with the Risen One.[9]

The prophets and Jesus showcase a new way to imagine how the world can be, and they are unencumbered by worldly consciousness. Jewish rabbi and theologian Abraham Joshua Heschel says that the prophets bring about this new order because their vision is aligned with God's vision: "The prophet is a [human] who sees the world with the eyes of God, and in the sight of God even things of beauty or acts of ritual are an abomination when associated with injustice."[10] Prophets are not simply proclaimers of justice and compassion, as if they are speaking "in the name of moral law." Rather, they speak on behalf of the "God of justice, for God's concern for justice."[11]

Like Brueggemann, Heschel tells us that the very rationality of the world is in stark contrast with the way of God, expressed by the prophets. He says, "What is most rational to the prophets seems irrational to us."[12] "Because as Christians we ally ourselves with this God, and we are no longer operating with the understanding of the world; how we act is foolish to our worldly detractors. This is why Paul tells us in Romans 12 that we must no longer conform to the patterns of this world; why in 1 Corinthians he calls the cross "foolishness," why he proclaims to the Philippians the peace of God that "surpasses all understanding." God is operating with a different framework, undoing the reality and the consciousness that we dwell in.

This new consciousness, though, is not meant to merely allow us to transcend our present suffering, but to engage with it materially, without fear or mindfulness of worldly political constraints, because we are assured of the coming victory of Jesus. We serve a God who has defeated death, and thus our politics are oriented toward defeating death. Our prophetic imaginations allow us to name as practical what the world calls impractical; what they call impossible, we call possible; because we serve a God who rules over all of the worldly political orders, and subverts them with God's political order.

For us to bring about this new consciousness, we must interrogate what dominates our current consciousness. To consider how we are dominated, we need to think of the underlying assumptions in our society that go without saying.

Looking to where we find bipartisan agreement gives us a clue into discovering such assumptions; we are searching for the foregone conclusions of our society in which we find no notable or substantive disagreement. Prophetic imagination allows us to challenge, critique, and demonstrate an alternative to those conclusions.

Here we can find three things that fundamentally order us: neoliberalism, Whiteness, and violence. They are similar to what Martin Luther King Jr. called the three evils of society: materialism, racism, and militarism.[13] There are others, but any serious challenge of these three ideas is seemingly politically impractical because these evils are forgone conclusions of our society. They are so preeminent, so dominating, that they act as lords in our society, when Jesus should be Lord. This is precisely why the consciousness that maintains them must be dismantled, and why placing Jesus in the highest political office allows us to not bow to Caesar, if you will. When we declare that we have no king but Christ, we can challenge the other kings of the world and their consciousness, too.

First, let's start with neoliberalism. Though neoliberalism describes a specific school of thought, one that values so-called "evidence-based" policy, it makes assumptions about the supremacy of the market economy and capitalism. George Monbiot, writing for *The Guardian*, described the preeminence of neoliberalism like this: "We appear to accept the proposition that this utopian, millenarian faith describes a neutral force; a kind of biological law, like Darwin's theory of evolution. But the philosophy arose as a conscious attempt to reshape human life and shift the locus of power."[14]

In an article for *Current Affairs*, journalist and political theorist Nathan Robinson demonstrates how neoliberalism worms itself into our minds, arguing that the shared values of our society go unchallenged under neoliberalism, but the political parties merely disagree about how to achieve them:

> Republicans argue that their tax cut will increase GDP, reduce the deficit, and reduce taxes for the middle class. Democrats reply that the tax cut will not increase GDP, will not reduce the deficit, and will not reduce the middle-class's tax burden. Both parties are arguing around a shared premise: The goal is to cut taxes for the middle class, reduce the deficit, and grow GDP.[15]

This outlook assumes the value of growth, protecting market interests, and making us better (read: more productive) workers. The dialogue centers on how to achieve those things, which we see as fundamental goods. It instills in our minds the value of preparing individuals for success in the market.

Jesus offers a counterconsciousness to this in the Sermon on the Mount when he says that "no one can serve two masters," that we "cannot serve God and wealth" (Matthew 6:24). If neoliberalism, that is to say market-oriented thinking, shapes our imagination, we cannot also claim it to be informed by Jesus. Immediately following that portion of the sermon, Jesus admonishes his listeners not to worry. The context of worrying here is related to immediate needs. He goes on to say, "Do not worry about your life, what you will eat or what you will drink, or about your body, what you will wear." Trusting that God will provide is exactly the alternative consciousness that confronts neoliberal thinking. Jesus encourages his listeners to "strive first for the kingdom of God and his righteousness [or justice][16] and all these things will be given to you as well" (Matthew 6:25–33).

How does the church demonstrate that trust in God's provision? We see an example in the Church of Jerusalem in Acts 2. Luke tells us, "All who believed were together and had all things in common; they would sell their possessions and goods and distribute the proceeds to all, as any had need" (vv. 43–45). And again in Acts 4:34, "There was not a needy person among them, for as many as owned lands or houses sold them and brought the proceeds of what was sold." The church is demonstrating an alternative economy and way of thinking about money and markets—that consciousness disrupts the way the dominant frame infects our imaginations. We have to confront the dominant economic frame of neoliberalism and see where it has invaded our minds.

Neoliberal ideology imagines solutions to our problems as market-based and as only needing a minimal amount of government intervention (so it should not be confused with market essentialism, the idea that advocates for unfettered market capitalism). It argues that with just enough course correction from the state, the market can be the force that brings all of us equity and prosperity. It argues that human progress, growth, and production need never be limited for the sake of equality, justice, or to prevent environmental devastation.

At the root of neoliberalism, economic liberty is equated with true liberty. So it ultimately became the force that was victorious over communism in the Cold War, along with being the force that currently fights trade and public unions, regulation, and taxing the wealthy—all of which are seen as an affront to individual liberty. Neoliberalism poses an affront to the public and common good in favor of individualism and privatization.

Neoliberals believe that the market will solve all our problems, and when it doesn't, it only needs minor regulation. Their answer to a housing crisis? Deregulate housing so that developers will build more, as opposed to building affordable housing or requiring developers to pay into funds to build affordable housing. Their answer to job security? Not unions, but allowing for market competition to create the strongest jobs. Their answer to income inequality? Not taxing corporations, but rather allowing tax breaks so that they can reinvest income and provide more jobs.

This ideology says it is not good enough to simply change how we behave for the sake of love, but demands that we demonstrate how a love of others benefits us, benefits the market, and propels growth and progress. Without a fundamental change in what we value and how we consume, existentially pressing matters cannot be meaningfully addressed and transformed.

However, the most pressing concern that neoliberalism fails to address meaningfully is climate change, which must be an area of urgent concern for Christians, who are called to steward creation, preserve life, and at the very least, extend human flourishing. Naming the market, and market-based growth, as an essential good limits how we can combat climate change. If we only use market forces to combat it, we won't make drastic enough changes to eliminate the use of fossil fuels at the rate that we must to combat the warming of our planet, because the most important and effective tools may not be the most profitable in the short term.

The 2021 report from the International Panel on Climate Change suggested that for the next thirty years the planet would continue to warm if we don't zero out *all* fossil fuel emissions in the next decade. Further, we need to develop technologies that "suck vast quantities of carbon dioxide back out of the atmosphere." Not only will this require the development of technology at a staggering rate,[17] but it also requires the political will to combat the neoliberalist approach that, if unchallenged, will continue to pump carbon emissions into the air for the sake of economic prosperity. Its solutions create circumstances where individuals (and corporations) do not have a moral responsibility to change their behavior, because the market compels them to change on its own. So a corporation can keep running as usual, making choices with the bottom line in mind rather than environmental urgency, because something like a carbon tax will eventually make the price of carbon prohibitively expensive to use. Climate change thus becomes one consumer choice. Faced with the slow change of market-based solutions, the changes that occur in the long run, neoliberalism shifts the anxiety around climate change to individuals, leaving both lawmakers and corporations off the hook.

Instead of seeking structural solutions that also change minds and hearts, we turn to relationships and empathy as a way to make long-lasting change. But because systemic issues are often difficult to observe and even more difficult to measure and combat in relation to immediate profit, appealing to individuals is bound to fail. More than structural change, we need a spiritual and religious change, because we are dealing with, quite frankly, a spiritual and religious force in neoliberalism—a force that captivates our imaginations and transforms our behavior. This religious change isn't rooted in personal conversion, because "Jesus is Lord" is not just a personal confession—it is a political reordering.

Just as neoliberalism frames our economic order, Whiteness defines our racial order. Whiteness here does not simply mean white skin, but rather, the meaning we attach to white skin, which organizes all of us racially. Put another way, my brown skin has meaning to it because when white skin is seen as superior, it diminishes the value of non-white skin. Our skin colors exist before they are assigned an essence and before they are assigned *meaning*.

Race, then, does not have *inherent* value that is permanent or essential to us. However, the lack of inherent value does not rule out race having *intrinsic* value, meaning that it contextually belongs. Whiteness pervades our society so much that from the minute we are born, our skin color is assigned meaning. Race is fundamentally about how someone looks and not a self-professed identity. So individuals do not decide their race, it is decided for them by the powers—by Whiteness itself.

Theologian Willie James Jennings names Whiteness as emerging out of Christianity, thereby making Whiteness an order that is brought to our society by Christians (even though it is fundamentally antithetical to the life and ministry of Jesus of Nazareth). Through colonialism, missionary work, and the spread of Christianity by Europeans, Whiteness and Christianity were spread together. Without doing the work to separate the two, it almost didn't matter how well-intentioned European Christians were—they brought their race, as well as their faith, wherever they went.

Jennings says that Whiteness "designates white bodies" as beautiful, good, and truthful—and encourages everyone, including people of color, to assess themselves and their value through it. Whiteness isn't just a group of people, it's "an invitation, a becoming, a transformation, an accomplishment." I can speak to this as a child of immigrants, because I actively shed the Egyptian, Arab, and Brown aspects of my life to try to relate more closely to Whiteness. For example, I mastered the White language, the White culture, and the White value system to assimilate into it. Whiteness organizes how we see the world and how we *are* in the world. Whiteness allows individuals to imagine themselves "as part of the central facilitating reality, the reality that makes sense of, interprets, organizes, and narrates the world." In a racialized society, Whiteness becomes synonymous with goodness and creates a hierarchy based on that goodness.[18]

Although racial hierarchy is imposed upon us, prophetic witness and imagination afford us the chance to cast a new vision and consciousness for humanity. But before we can do that, we must reckon with the impact of Whiteness and how it orders us—that is to say, we need to address racism in all of its forms before we try to live in a "post-racial" way.

Because Whiteness is embedded in and elemental to our society, we do not automatically detect it. Whiteness is assumed, and so it is rarely noted. Naming the reality and impact of race—for example, Black History Month, or prioritizing hiring to overcome prejudice via affirmation action, or even educating students via a lens of racism—is often met with resistance or even claims of racism. In such cases, the Whiteness that is being subverted by these efforts is often not readily observable to White people, or even to people of color. It takes consciousness to observe where Whiteness resides in our society. To overcome Whiteness or racial ordering, we need to see both where it infiltrates our society and the power structures that uphold it.

Everyone who does not actively resist this racial hierarchy defaults to maintaining it. This includes non-White individuals when they try to promote themselves in the racial hierarchy instead of resisting it, thereby perpetuating Whiteness. Playing into the systems of Whiteness is an invariable part of survival, so we need to rely not just on individual consciousness but also collective consciousness to overcome it.

In the United States, racialized chattel slavery fundamentally shaped the nation around Whiteness. The scars of slavery continue to impact the fabric of the nation and the opportunities for Black individuals. We see its effect in law enforcement, as well as in our criminal justice system. Black and Latino folks disproportionately make up a greater share of prisoners than they do the general population. As of 2019, Latino people make up 16 percent of the population, and 23 percent of the prison population; Black people make up 12 percent of the general population, and 33 percent of the prison population. In contrast, White people make up 64 percent of the population, and just 30 percent of the prison population.[19]

Despite a majority of Americans believing that police are racially biased, a larger percentage of Americans still trust the police.[20] But police unions and other legal protections make reform very difficult, and racial targeting still results in the disproportionate arrest and killing of Black people. We know these systems maintain Whiteness because of how viscerally movements surrounding prison abolition and defunding the police are met with massive resistance, even among people of color. So while most Americans agree reform is necessary, reform alone is politically challenging and insufficient in changing consciousness prophetically. Abolition or defunding is a more direct confrontation of the Whiteness that law enforcement maintains, yet too many in power, both liberals and conservatives, see it as politically unviable and unrealistic. Abolishing the police or defunding the police suggests a reimagining of how to keep our communities safe. It is rooted in asking questions about how community safety and law enforcement work. So while reform is a good step, it does not confront the consciousness of the world as much as a complete reimagination does.

The defunding or abolition of law enforcement does not undo Whiteness, entirely, but the resistance to these ideas tells us something about how Whiteness orders us. Because our political apparatus only advances causes that it believes are popular and viable, we know that we need another order to challenge the current one. The institutions that maintain this order are protected at all costs because damaging them existentially results in *disordering.*

Jesus calls us to reimagine the ways that our world orders us. Jesus disrupted social norms, even those attached to ethnicity, in his time. He included foreigners and outsiders in the fold. Famously, he demonstrates this when he tells the story of the Good Samaritan, where a Samaritan helps a Jewish person, while fellow Jews ignore him. The relationship and enmity between Jews and Samaritans is a storied and long-lasting one, yet Jesus disrupts it by extending our definition of neighbors.

Finally, we turn to violence as another part of collective consciousness that is so common and foundational that it can be hard to notice. Philosopher and theologian Jacques Ellul, who was a foremost thinker on nonviolence, tells us, "Every state is founded on violence and cannot maintain itself save by and through violence."[21] All of our laws are fundamentally backed by the threat of violence, and so our actions are based out of fear. It may be challenging to see why something like a speed limit is backed by the threat of violence, but we largely follow the rules of the road so that we don't collect tickets. The order of our society is kept because we fear punishment or retribution if we don't follow the rules. Sometimes the rules are sensible enough that we are intrinsically motivated to follow them, but even then it is violence that may be ordering our sensibilities.

When the state demonstrates flagrant violence, with war or with police brutality, we are more likely to become aware of this, but we often tolerate it because we are afraid of the violent repercussions of speaking out or taking action against the violence of the state.

Countering violence with violence does not reorder our consciousness, but rather reconfigures state power and violence. Governments stay in power "by violence, simply by violence."[22] The state's monopoly on violence is the only way it can protect its citizens from other forms of violence,[23] with violence being "the sole means available to those in power," "to claim their rights." Ellul says that Jesus knew how this worked, too, citing his words in Matthew 20:25: "You know that the rulers of the Gentiles lord it over them, and their great ones are tyrants over them." Ellul argues that Jesus is not just describing monarchs and "controllers of wealth" but anyone who is in leadership. According to Ellul, there is no way for someone to stay in power except through violence.[24]

We cannot imagine security and safety without violence. We cannot imagine a world without owners, supervisors, and managers. We submit to a violent hierarchy because, while an alternative would be great, some might say it's just not practical in this day and age. They argue that we would be overrun by more violence if not for the state, yet that is precisely how violence gets perpetuated. We struggle to imagine new ways to keep our communities safe because violence is all we have known. We struggle to imagine a world without retributive violence because we are programmed to respond with violence.

This is why when Representative Barbara Lee voted against the U.S. invasion of Afghanistan, she was ridiculed and shamed as anti-American. In a sense, to oppose violence is indeed to be anti-American and anti-state. After twenty years of futile occupation, Lee was proven right, but that doesn't change the fact that she was the only one to oppose the war.[25] She was not vindicated as a result, because when a prophet is proven right, lamentation, not victory, follows.

Even as we recognize that neoliberalism, Whiteness, and violence are shaping our ways of being, the church can be free of such constraints on our imaginations because we serve Jesus as Lord. But this is no easy task. It takes a lot of undoing, since we tend to see the state as responsible for the common good and the common order. Our society is presented to us as a given, and any challenge to its order is often seen as opposition not just to the state, but to goodness altogether, because without Jesus it is these assumptions that frame what goodness is.

Theologian William Cavanaugh argues that the church marginalizes itself by abdicating its role in demonstrating and advocating for the common good to the state.[26] Daniel Bell, a sociologist who wrote influential books on post-industrial society, argues that the church gave ground to the state by allowing it to hold the office of "chief social actor:"

> We are used to thinking of the state as the chief social actor. Even those who espouse the currently popular view that the state should have a smaller economic footprint do not really relinquish politics as statecraft insofar as they do not really want the state to surrender its supervisory control of society; rather, they want it to enforce policies that protect and preserve the market.[27]

Bell showcases that both neoliberalism and violence organize how we relate to the state, and organize how we advocate for action. I do believe political action in that violent and neoliberal environment is entirely necessary, but it should never replace our prophetic imagination and our demonstration of another way of being, a "counterconsciousness," as Brueggemann puts it.

The church can be an example of a community that throws off the constraints of violence, neoliberalism, and Whiteness. We can demonstrate that another world is possible. However, we can do so only when we interrogate how thinking and ways of the world have infiltrated our churches, because they invariably have. We cannot swim in this water without getting wet, so to speak. It is not good enough to simply deny the fact that we are saturated—we need to "dry off." We need to live into and model a way of repentance from these worldly sins.

Only then can we cast a vision for what the world could be like, free from the consciousness of the world. We then can show that it is indeed possible, on this side of heaven, to live in another way. Our communities can model the practicality of what our political apparatus names as impractical. We know that more is possible because we relate to a God who shows us an entirely new way of doing things through God's presence and God incarnate, Jesus.

God's counterconsciousness is a refutation of the consciousness of the world, a refutation of neoliberalism, Whiteness, and violence. When faced with an oppressive economic order, God frees the captives in Israel and promises liberation to the oppressed. God, through Jesus on the cross, doesn't count our debts against us but instead frees us from their burden. When faced with an ethnic hierarchy, God disrupts it by welcoming the stranger, advocating for the outcast, and relating to the other, while rebuking those who don't. When faced with violence, Jesus submits himself to its ultimate end, death, and then defeats death once and for all. The political and economic consequences of the work of God are an affront to the ways of the world, and we must allow them to embolden us into imagining new ways to live and relate.

Chapter 11

Practicality in Partnership with Imagination

Prophetic imagination opens up a path for the church to counter the imagination-constraining consciousness of the world with a beautiful alternative. The lordship of Christ shapes a vision for humanity that is rooted in the promises of the age to come, realized in the present moment, as we follow the will of God "on earth as it is in heaven." The radical, imaginative politics that this opens up uproots us from our present circumstances and allows us to consider an otherwise unthinkable world.

But a significant challenge remains: how do we do this in the present age, when political engagement consistently asks us to compromise this prophetic vision? It is impossible to participate in a state-sanctioned political process and bring about this sort of world-changing vision—the goals of the two are fundamentally opposed. So then, how can one be motivated by this God-given vision yet engage in something that so thoroughly pales in comparison?

Some Christians approach this by trying to create an alternative community that makes change by modeling from within that another world is possible. However, that raises the question of the purpose of the church. If our goal is only to act differently within our ecclesial bodies in order to demonstrate to the world how it can make a change, we'll either be ineffective or imperialistic. Ineffective, because small churches just don't have the platform or reach to allow their alternative example to impact change in the world, and also because that incredibly passive approach could easily be sidelined or ignored. Imperialistic, because we may try to impose our way on the rest of the world through violence and coercion.

Apolitical churches that "seek to be the change they want to see in the world" by ignoring or setting aside politics are often being led by people whose lives are not largely impacted by their political inaction. What happens politically is immaterial to the bodies of their members (or perhaps their leaders, mainly), and so it's not important to them to set an example of political engagement. They tend to see their role as providing an alternative that is completely separate from the world, so lack of political engagement becomes a virtue.

But many of these churches are also resistant to interrogating the way the world has shaped them. It is not good enough to name ourselves as an alternative, as counterconscious, without interrogating how the systems of the world have infiltrated our churches. When we think of our churches as "pure" institutions without questioning where they are complicit in worldly patterns of sin, we are what Jesus calls "whitewashed tombs," clean on the outside and full of dirty bones on the inside (Matthew 23:27–28). If we don't interrogate how our society has not only affected our churches but reordered them according to sexual, gendered, racial, able-bodied, and economic hierarchies, we haven't effectively overpowered the strong man, to use Jesus' terms.

In Luke 11, Jesus exorcises a demon out of a person who couldn't speak, and the person is healed. Jesus' detractors claimed he was casting out demons in the name of "Beelzebul, the rulers of the demons." However Jesus pointed out their impossible accusation—"A kingdom divided against itself can't stand." In this we are empowered to exorcise our demons—that is to say, homophobia, sexism, racism, ableism, and classism—lest our house fall. We cannot expect to stay standing if we preach that Jesus is Lord, while we in turn submit to lords of the world.

Jesus' interest, then and now, is in combatting the forces of death and darkness in the world, and he is intent on plundering them. For Jesus, his lordship has political connotations that cannot and should not be limited to the walls of a church or the boundaries of the community. We're all called to counter the forces of death in our church and in the world at large.

Jesus invites us to partake in this vision for the world, not just in our communities, but also outside of them. We do this for the sake of the expression of the gospel, for the declaration that Jesus is Lord, and also for the sake of disciple-making. Especially for Christians committed to evangelism, it is the responsibility of the church to express the gospel in earnest, in the world. And fundamentally, expressing the gospel earnestly in the world includes political involvement as we seek to eradicate evil systems and liberate the oppressed.

On the other end of the spectrum, many radical Christians think that anything that upholds the status quo or the current order perpetuates oppression, and we should therefore eschew participating at all. Others think that engaging in something like voting or activism makes us unclean, because politics is a violent and self-interested process. In both of these cases, we find a thin line between prophecy and cynicism. Is it possible to hold the eschatological vision of what is possible on one hand, while on the other hand, actively participating in politics as the gospel compels us? Can we be both prophetic and pragmatic? Both imaginative and industrious? Both "wise as serpents and innocent as doves" (Matthew 10:16)?

The answer to this question lies in how we see one another via the work of Jesus on the cross and the promise of the age to come. As we await our full liberation, we still must do what we can to advance the gospel. Though the forces of death have met their end, we advocate against them now. Though the battle against sin is ultimately won, we still struggle against it daily. Though we are assured salvation in the age to come, we bring heaven to earth in the present age.

The crucifixion of Jesus fulfilled all of God's justice by making rights wrong and by ending sin and death once and for all. In his resurrection, and his dwelling on earth after his resurrection, Jesus showed us that we are not only promised to resurrect with him, but that we can make a difference now, that we can help change the world here on earth. The church is charged with a mission and a life on earth that matters.

Sadly, for much of Christian history, Christians have taken that charge and twisted it to pursue their own self-interested ends as they pillaged the earth and conquered land. They certainly acted politically, but with their political interests in mind rather than the interests of the oppressed. We see the same phenomenon in the United States, as the Republican Party and White Evangelicalism have become fused—in fact, White Evangelicalism grew under Trump as his supporters increasingly adopted the label.[1] It is sad, but appears to be true, that many Evangelicals here are ignoring the political demands of the gospel to side with the oppressed, for their own benefit and to grow their power.

Understandably, these self-serving politics of not only Evangelicals, but also European colonists before them, tempt many Christians to remain apolitical. What dominant Christians did throughout history was a misapplication of the earnest expression of the gospel and had disastrous consequences, but their actions do not give us reason to abandon our responsibility to love our neighbors today.

Apolitical Christians often point to Romans 13, Paul's famous passage that commands Christians to submit to governing authorities. For many, this passage may be an indictment of the entire thesis of this book, but I want to explore it because, in my reading, it *charges* us to act politically, instead of advising us against doing so. So I want to briefly visit the text, even if a full analysis might be another book altogether.

> Let every person be subject to the governing authorities; for there is no authority except from God, and those authorities that exist have been instituted by God. Therefore whoever resists authority resists what God has appointed, and those who resist will incur judgment. For rulers are not a terror to good conduct, but to bad. Do you wish to have no fear of the authority? Then do what is good, and you will receive its approval; for it is God's servant for your good. But if you do what is wrong, you should be afraid, for the authority does not bear the sword in vain! It is the servant of God to execute wrath on the wrongdoer. (Romans 13:1–7)

We must first consider the occasion of the passage. Paul was writing to a persecuted church plant in Rome. He may very well have been advising the Christians in Rome not to rock the boat over the injustice of the Roman Empire, which had the power to wipe out his small church's effort. Additionally, some have speculated that the members of the household of Caesar, who might have found comfort in this passage, also grasped its radical political meaning—Paul was naming God as the ruler of the authorities, and saying those authorities must obey God, who ordered them.[2]

Paul is not telling us to submit blindly to the state; he certainly did not in his own life. By planting a church in Rome, Paul had already acknowledged he was not submitting to the empire, but rather rebelling against it. Further, Paul, and most of the New Testament writers (and Jesus, as well!) died at the hands of the state as political dissidents.

By naming God as the arranger of the government, Paul co-opts the power of other gods the Romans thought instituted the powers, like Mars or Jupiter, or any of the pantheon that have been introduced to the civic mythology. Paul names the God and Father of the crucified Christ as the authority, and his call for the Roman church to respect authority then was ultimately about respecting God, not those authorities established by earthly kingdoms. Here's how Karl Barth put it:

> The mighty powers that be are measured by reference to God, as are all human, temporal, concrete things. God is their beginning and end, their justification and their condemnation, their 'Yes' and their 'No.' If we adopt an attitude of revolution toward them—and this is the attitude adopted in the Epistle of the Romans, as is shown by the unmistakable fact that the passive dealing with human *rulers* follows immediately after the passage dealing with the *enemy* and is prefaced by the quite clear statement that men are to overcome *evil*.[3]

Romans 13 must be read in light of the rest of the book of Romans as well as the entire New Testament, which offers us a clear narrative of the lordship of Jesus: he is our political ruler, first, and foremost. Romans is read in light of this revelation, and in chapter 1 of the epistle, Paul declares the power and the righteousness of God, a threat and a counter to Rome and the power of Caesar.[4] When we get to chapter 12, the audience is called to be a radical alternative to the world and to express that radicality in earnest.

From Romans 12:2: "Do not be conformed to this world, but be transformed by the renewing of your minds, so that you may discern what is the will of God—what is good and acceptable and perfect." Paul was asking us to be transforming agents in the world, not ones that conform to the world. We are to be change agents, according to the will of God.

In verses 9–10, Paul admonishes his audience to have real love, real mutuality, and to honor one another: "Let love be genuine; hate what is evil, hold fast to what is good; love one another with mutual affection; outdo one another in showing honor." Paul was interested in rejecting the ways the world has given our bodies meaning and in creating a new humanity, one ordered by God. This is a deeply political statement that has political consequences in the world, as well.

Then in verses 17–18, he writes, "Do not repay anyone evil for evil, but take thought for what is noble in the sight of all. If it is possible, so far as it depends on you, live peaceably with all." He is offering us an ethic by which to live: don't practice vengeance, but spread love and peaceable living. So politically, we are to help create circumstances where love and peace thrive, which means, in part, that we need to act politically *for* love and peace, and against hatred and violence.

Romans 13 is not the Bible's central teaching on the state. Though the text clearly recognizes the reality of worldly power, a closer examination of context and translation choices reveals that the reading of Romans 13 as God's blessing of earthly powers is at best a stretch.

The word in Romans 13:1 where much of our discussion lies is *tassō* (τάσσω), which the NRSV translates as "instituted," the KJV as "ordains," the NIV as "established." Within its context it appears as *tetagmenai* (τεταγμέναι). It "derives from military use, meaning *arranged* [my emphasis] in rank and file."[5] It can be translated in a variety of ways: "appoint," "order," "arrange," "lay down."[6]. It could also mean "place" or "station" of a person or thing in a fixed spot; it can also mean "put someone over or in charge of someone or something," or even "to be put under someone's control."[7] What we find is that the word has a lot of variation in its translation and is hard to translate precisely. N.T. Wright translates it as "put in place,"[8] and so does the CEB. Interestingly enough, David Bentley Hart's translation is "subordinated,"[9] which is also a valid translation and brings about a much more complex possibility: the idea that God's rulership is above the state's. I favor "put in place," or "order."

We see in this that God is not creating, instituting, or ordaining these earthly powers. Perhaps God is ordering them, like a librarian cataloging books, but God does not "approve" of those books, necessarily. Amy-Jill Levine notes, "It is difficult to understand how Paul would sanction either the Roman empire as instituted, or 'arranged by God;' the present age is 'night,' 'darkness' (v. 12), and 'evil,' from which people need to be freed (cf. Gal. 1:4, 1 Thess. 5:3; 2 Thess. 2:6–12)."[10]

In fact, as we pursue a true nonviolent alternative, we are stuck with the reality of government and the ruling powers. So rather than pining for an alternative that does not yet exist, we do what we can now to make a practical change. Unlike the church in Rome, it is not our job to merely submit to the state, but rather to effect change, because we have been given the authority to do that—by God, yes, but also by the state. We participate in a liberal democracy, and according to Romans 13, we are in fact responsible for doing this! If Western democracies are indeed by the people and for the people, individuals are the God-ordered authorities. We may bear a responsibility to influence and affect our government because of how it is ordered, but more than that, we are compelled by love to participate in practical ways now.

Loving our neighbors, then, is at the heart of the gospel and should inspire our political action. Though we should prophesy a counterconsciousness to the way of the world, we do not refuse any hope of immediate and immanent progress because of that greater goal. Cynicism cannot guide our political inaction—we are moved to do whatever we can now, to alleviate suffering, bring hope, and spread love in the world.

So as we bring new political imagination to the world, we discipline ourselves to influence the heads of state to advocate for the poor and oppressed and to love their neighbors. As a housing activist in Philadelphia, I often tell people that I am interested in everyone in Philadelphia having a house they can afford in a neighborhood that provides for their needs, because Jesus meant it when he said to love our neighbors. For me, that means doing what we can now to actually provide for the needs of our neighbors, and while I would love to revolutionize the racialized, violent, neoliberal order, I realize that that won't happen overnight. I do what I can now because the love of Christ moves and acts practically.

This not only means voting but also trying to influence the government in other ways. I participate in the Philadelphia Coalition For Affordable Communities, where we engage with Philadelphia's city council to put the land back in community hands, as we say. Our goal is to fund and support the development of affordable and accessible housing—we want development without displacement. Additionally, we advocate for green spaces for recreation and food production. Working with lawmakers and the mayor's office to make change is rather constraining and a far cry from the prophetic imagination. It involves meetings, phone calls, and organizing people. We work on building power so that lawmakers listen to us, and we learn to compromise to get something accomplished. We hold to our radical ideals of housing for everyone—advocating for housing as a human right—but because we live within the political constraints of the moment, we take the steps we need to take to advance our cause, conscious of the fact that we will have to make sacrifices along the way.

It can be easy to become cynical at this process, especially when we are up against forces that are much stronger than we are. It can be discouraging to work hard on legislation and fail because lawmakers hollowed it out, or won't bring it to a vote. It can be easy to see the incremental results and succumb to despair.

Sadly, cynicism and despair too often motivate political inaction more than a commitment to radical politics and change. People opposed to voting, for example, may decry participating in the system because that participation upholds the system, but on-the-ground activists know that inaction doesn't create change—even if that incremental change isn't revolutionary. Waiting—whether it's for a contemporary political revolution or, for Christians, the age to come—requires patience with the status quo, to an extent. But it is those with the least to lose who too often advocate against participation, either because they see it as compromising their purity or perpetuating an unjust system.

The political process is slow, at times seemingly designed to discourage participation as our attention span wanes. Our city council meetings, for example, occur on Thursday mornings, when many of the most affected are at work or school, which discourages public testimony. But earnest advocates see beyond these limits—they know that gradual change is better than no change at all. The powers upholding the status quo benefit from our inaction, and further, are indifferent toward a radical ideology that does little more than work in abstractions. So much time is lost on academic and intellectual debates that don't change our material circumstances. Those discussions are not unimportant, but if they prevent us from practical actions, the powers that be, the ones to whom Jesus is an affront, continue to hold all of their power. The status quo thrives on indifference, on apoliticality, and on politics that never leave the pages of the books they are written in.

The most practical activists and political actors compromise to move their agenda forward. And when compromise leads to success, they celebrate their win, instead of sulking in what could have been. The most progressive members of Congress campaign on progressive politics but invariably compromise their values, making less progress than they desire, but progress nevertheless. We may see them as selling out, but I think we need a reality check about our elected officials, whom we may idealize as revolutionaries. We're all better off if we "right-size" them, so to speak. We can expect them to operate within the basic parameters of our government because we are electing them to serve that very government. For Christians, so long as we understand that full liberation won't come through a constrained political process, we need to use the process we do have to love our neighbor further and make progress toward alleviating suffering.

So how does one practically engage in politics? In my experience, I have found helpful these four principles: be focused, organized, generous, and informed.

1. **Be Focused.** I spend most of my political and activist energy on housing. I care about and am interested in other issues, but I've been afforded an opportunity to work for housing justice and I seized it. Putting my effort into a single issue keeps me from spreading myself too thin. Further, advocating in local politics is often a better use of time than in state or national politics (though that is also important). Local politics is not nearly as sensationalized as national politics, but it is where our action may be the greatest. You might choose to use your time and efforts differently than me, but however you approach it, I do recommend investing your energy in a focused way.

2. **Be Organized.** Don't go it alone. Find a group that shares your area of interest and join them, or create your own. Try not to get lost on theoretical details— though those can be sorted through elsewhere—and look for people making a difference in policy. Doing this work in the community makes it more efficacious, more fun, and more sustainable. Being organized builds power, which is the currency of politics. A single letter written to a legislator is much weaker than one hundred of them, or better, one hundred phone calls to their office.

3. **Be Generous.** What you can't accomplish with your time and labor, perhaps you can accomplish with your money. Support campaigns of candidates you would vote for; donate to churches and organizations

doing the work you care about. This is especially helpful if you fund priorities you cannot personally commit to. Money, like power, is another currency of politics, and fundraising is a big part of it.

4. **Be Informed.** Stay alert about elections and inform yourself and others about them. Subscribe to a daily newspaper and a national newspaper, not only to inform yourself but also to encourage good reporting and discourage the misinformation that so greatly affects our politics. Commit yourself to learning about local, national, and global issues. Consider listening to perspectives from marginalized groups and allowing them to inform your politics. You don't need to know it all. Find trusted sources that you can lean on so you are not doing all of your own research, and consult experts you trust. For example, I ask my lawyer friends for their recommendations regarding which judges I should vote for. Rely on others you trust for information so that you don't overwhelm yourself.

If you feel stifled by gradualism, I understand. Incremental political progress may feel limiting to those of us who long for radical change, but this is why we need to be motivated by much more than our present political arrangement. What motivates us is the presence of God in our lives, who gives us the conviction to continue to enact love in the world. This is why we need to be disciplined to maintain our hope.

Chapter 12

The Disciplines of Anger and Hope

And the LORD was sorry that he had made humankind on the earth, and it grieved him to his heart.

Genesis 6:6

This is how the writer described God's emotion after God "saw that the wickedness of humankind was great in the earth, and that every inclination of the thoughts of their hearts was only evil continually" (v. 5). Immediately after this comes the great flood that wipes out the earth, save Noah's family.

This does not mean God is affected or moved by human emotions (though some argue this). In my view, God elects to be heartbroken at the sight of the evil in our world; it is God's own choice, not necessarily because human emotions have power over God. I find deep comfort in this emotional description of God, especially in the midst of my own pain and lamentation over injustice. God grieves evil, sin, and wickedness on earth, and as we gain proximity to God and to those who suffer because of this evil, we learn to empathize and connect with the pain of God.

Sharing in the pathos of God is what moves us to political action as Christians. When God is angry, we also are angry. When God is grieving, we join in grief. What God laments, we share in that lamentation. We empathize with the pathos of God, we empathize with the oppressed, and if we are oppressed ourselves, we learn to feel our pain and our trauma. We must enter into this grief to be able to recover, and face this pain to fully heal from and transform it.

Theologian Willie Jennings voiced the importance of *all of us* sharing in the righteous indignation of God in a podcast interview recording in response to the murder of George Floyd. Jennings described how friends had reached out to him to say that they "can't imagine" what he was feeling then. Jennings responded with, "Yes, you can." Because, as he said, "Anger is shareable." This idea can empower those in dominant social positions, such as White folks, to hold the anger of the oppressed instead of succumbing to what Jennings calls "the sickness of whiteness" that merely turns the powerful into gawkers and spectators of the pain of the marginalized.[1]

I was speaking recently to an Anabaptist pastor who suggested that anger, of any kind, was a sin. He said there was no such thing as "righteous anger" in the Bible. He added, "Every time anger is mentioned, especially in the New Testament, it's either mentioned with a grave warning or it's just called flat-out sin."[2] But the Bible is full of moments of righteous anger, through the Old and New Testaments, and in Ephesians, as this pastor pointed out, the writer admonishes us to, "Be angry but do not sin" (Ephesians 4:26).

Anger is not a sin, but what often follows—violence or hatred—is. In fact, as Jennings says, "Jesus stands between anger and hatred."[3] Because we too often link anger with violence and hatred, we do not allow ourselves to see the source of that anger, out of fear of where it may lead us. We may seek to avoid anger as a way to guard ourselves against the pain of our oppressed siblings, or, for the oppressed, the pain within ourselves. But our empathy with the righteous indignation of God leads us to confront the source of evil that disturbs us. That confrontation produces justice and hope.

When we do not allow ourselves space for anger, we miss the power of the righteous anger of God expressed through the Bible. God is righteously angry at oppression. God wiped out the earth in heartbreak when witnessing unending evil. God toppled the Red Sea onto Pharaoh and his chariots. God destroyed the prophets of Baal when they made a mockery of God. Jesus flipped over tables and drove out money changers who made the temple into a corrupt marketplace. The apostle Paul did not shy away from using the harshest of terms to describe those who exclude the vulnerable. There's no shortage of righteous anger in the Bible, and yet we see Christians who cannot bear to sympathize with the anger of the oppressed today.

Much of God's anger in the Bible is directed at injustice, and so ours should be, too. Many Christians try to erase God's anger from the Bible, and they consequently cannot empathize with Black anger today. We might start by empathizing with God, who empathizes with the oppressed. God is brokenhearted for the brokenhearted. God chooses to be in grief and God chooses the aggrieved to align with. This is what Paul means when he tells us to grieve with those who grieve, what Jesus means when he blesses those that mourn. God is aligned with the oppressed who lead us to grieve and lead us to rage against evil.

Too often the responsibility falls on the oppressed or their advocates to employ empathy as a means of transforming the oppressor. But in the face of oppression we must use our empathy to understand the plight of the oppressed so that we can confront the oppressor. Our empathy finds its source in the pathos of God, the God who empathizes with the oppressed, whose empathy the oppressed find comfort in.

Many Christians committed to nonviolence dismiss the so-called "God of the Old Testament," suggesting that God's wrath in the Old Testament is vastly different than the character of Jesus of Nazareth. But even a cursory overview of the Gospels shows that Jesus does not mince his words when it comes to wrath against oppressors.

Immediately after Peter rightfully names Jesus as the Messiah in Mark 8, Jesus predicts his own death. Peter, who expected a different sort of political liberator, rebukes Jesus, and in response Jesus names Peter "Satan." Jesus then declares that we must lose our lives to save them, "For what will it profit them to gain the whole world and forfeit their life?" (Mark 8:27–38).

After this demonstration of the cruciform, or cross-shaped, posture—the one rooted in humility, in the last being first—Jesus continues his journey to Capernaum, and along the way his disciples get into an argument about who is the greatest among them (Mark 9:33–37). They had just heard Jesus' words about his upside-down kingdom, but his disciples missed the moment and begin jockeying for social position. Jesus asks them what they are talking about and they remain silent—it is as if they are regressing in their understanding. Even Peter does not speak up.

Jesus once again tells them, "Whoever wants to be first must be last of all and servant of all." He then picks up a lowly child, who would have been overlooked and discarded in the household code of their day. He centers the child—displacing the disciples—and tells them that if they accept this child, they accept Jesus, and if they accept Jesus, they accept the Father who sent Jesus. Jesus, incredibly, identifies with the most marginalized, in the child, and the most exalted in the "one who sent him," whom he calls the Father. Jesus, in his very incarnation, bound himself to the lowliest and also the highest. It is this sort of proximity to the marginalized and to God that Jesus is calling us to.

When the child appears again later in the chapter, it is Jesus' wrath that expresses itself. He tells his disciples, "If any of you put a stumbling block before one of these little ones who believe in me, it would be better for you if a great millstone were hung around your neck and you were thrown into the sea" (Mark 9:42). Jesus' strong language here may not be comfortable for a particular type of peace-loving Christians who want to mute God's anger and wrath, but Jesus doesn't shy away from it, and neither should we. When we ignore it, we lose the opportunity to share in the rage of God as we witness injustice now. We are not faithful when we don't share in the fury. Jesus reserved his harshest words for those who caused the marginalized to stumble, and we should do the same.

God's wrath is never God's final answer, in any part of the Bible, because we are promised that God's love endures forever. God's love is longer than God's wrath. But God's wrath is rooted in God's love of the oppressed. God's wrath, on the cross, is poured out onto death, onto sin, and makes things right. God's love endures forever.

Through this lens, we might learn to read and understand retribution in the Bible. Because the powers that be, the very powers that our political action confronts, often use violence to achieve their ends, it is understandable to recoil at the violence in the Bible. Christians trying to move on from Christian supremacy, which has tied itself to the power of the state, are thus often suspicious of the violence and anger in the Bible. Put into the wrong hands, it could very well be devastating.

But the anger and wrath of God in the Bible is focused on oppressors; it should be read as a warning to oppressive Christians now, not a license for violence. A retributive God, one who confronts those who harm the oppressed, who warns that they would be better off tossed into the Sea of Galilee with a millstone hung around their neck than the judgment that awaits them, is a comfort to the oppressed. For the original audience of the Deuteronomistic History (the books of Deuteronomy through Kings), who were in Babylonian exile, a retributive God, one who would pour wrath out on their oppressors, was a reminder of God's faithfulness, of God's enduring love, of death not having the final answer. So it moves us today, when we encounter injustice, to empathize with God's anger and the shared anger of the oppressed.

But in judging the anger of the oppressed—for example, condemning the protests that have followed acts of police violence—we are missing the opportunity to empathize and to *imagine* what the oppressed are suffering from. Pastor and author Osheta Moore writes, "To be Black in America is never to be allowed to fully grieve." When she heard White people asking "Why do Black people always tear up their neighborhoods," or when she was told she was overreacting for sharing an eight-minute video of herself crying while speaking about Philando Castile because she didn't know him personally, she concluded: "You don't know how to honor Black grief."[4] We must see and respond to the grief of the oppressed by sharing that experience. The oppressed know that God feels our grief, and it is essential for allies standing by to enter into it.

What Moore and Jennings are saying is that if you do not feel grief and anger at the harm caused to those around you, you are not paying attention to what God is paying attention to. What I am saying is that if you do not politically commit and engage on the side of the oppressed, you cannot say you empathize with the grief and anger of God or of the oppressed. Shared anger is a spiritual discipline. Without moving to action, we cannot claim to empathize with the grief of God, whose heart breaks at the evil in humanity. Our political action demonstrates our shared anger and shared grief in a tangible way, using the tools we have at our disposal.

Allowing this anger and grief to inform our political commitments and action ensures that our politics are on the side of Jesus, who sides with the oppressed. Our anger is satisfied in justice, in righteousness. We see it perfectly on the cross, and we try to enact it as a church now, as we wait for it to come to fullness. In our political economy, though, it is often through gradualism and incrementalism that we see justice slowly achieved. But political action and results are not enough to satisfy that anger. We must be motivated by greater hope. Without that, the political process can often lead to even more anger, which can turn to hatred, violence, cynicism, and despair. Without a greater hope, we're at risk of embracing violence as a means for change, succumbing to cynicism, and pursuing a politics of personal gain.

My cynicism and despair almost overtook me recently. I started this book by sharing the events of a January 2017 love feast where Trump's ban on Muslim immigration led me to offer communion in light of that oppression, with the hope that God would save me yet again from my oppressors. The Trump years were some of the worst years of national politics in U.S. history and in my life. Joe Biden promised to be different. He ran his campaign on a moral referendum of Donald Trump's policies. Notably, Trump's family separation policy in response to immigration at the Mexican border was the height of his administration's evils. Jeff Sessions, the attorney general at the time, "told the prosecutors, 'we need to take away the children.'"[5] The scenes we saw at the border were something that Joe Biden promised to end. He was a moral leader, we were promised.

Yet less than a year into his presidency, we saw Haitian migrants being rounded up by U.S. Border Patrol on horseback, using the reins of horses as a whip. Joe Biden condemned the behavior, the media reported on it, and human rights groups were incensed. And in my heart, I was devastated, because I thought Biden would make things different for immigrants. I thought he would make things more just. Was all the work to unseat Trump worth it? Is politics just a sham? Is there any good that can come from it? This sort of hypocrisy is devastating to political engagement. It is challenging to keep people motivated to make incremental changes when these are the results. The progress is often slow, the setbacks are frequent, and victory is often a compromise.

As we take painstaking steps toward progress, the obstacles in our way can feel too great to overcome. It can be easy to be overwhelmed, to feel like we are in a small boat in a vast sea. Our political processes will too often expose the worst in our fellow humans, and that may tempt us to run from political engagement altogether. We may want to believe that we can side with and align with the oppressed in other ways than direct political action and participation, since the effects of such participation can be slow, ineffectual, and sometimes even boring. But that leaves politics in the hands of the oppressor.

We need to resist our cynicism and despair as we allow our discipline of anger to move us toward the discipline of hope.

Here's the truth, though. If we engage in politics merely on a superficial level, we can see the images of these brutalized Haitians and believe the two immigration policies are the same. But they are not, and progress is being made. Though we must be horrified at the treatment of our Haitian siblings, and though we need to hold Biden to account, it appears like Biden has restructured ICE (U.S. Immigration and Customs Enforcement) and moved well away from Trump's zero-tolerance policy. That is progress. It does not feel rewarding. It does not satisfy my anger. I am still angry and I still want more change. But noting any progress on behalf of the oppressed is essential for keeping our anger from turning to despair.

But the righteous indignation of God, the one we empathize with, the one who is aligned with the oppressed and motivates our political action, doesn't end with political participation. We participate in politics to advance change now. We participate with hope, with the belief that change is possible.

Christians know change is possible because we are assured that the battle against death is already over. We know that Jesus fulfilled the righteousness of God. We know that wrongs have been made right and are being made right. Our transcendent hope keeps us going today. But that hope, that discipline of hope, as Willie Jennings calls it, is in God, not in politics.

We may think that victory over death looks like a piece of legislation being passed. What may motivate us to advocate for that bill may be our hope in God's promises and the transformation God has brought into our lives, but God's hope is not fully expressed in a new law, a newly elected official, or any sort of political progress.

That's the dance we're doing: we are motivated by the transcendent in order to enact the immanent. Jesus showed us this on earth. In his ministry, Jesus consistently advocated for the oppressed and freed them. He healed people, he fed them, and he asked his disciples to care for them. He alleviated suffering in the immediate, but that good work was never mistaken for the salvific event of salvation found in Jesus' crucifixion and resurrection.

While Jesus is present to the moment, he also sees beyond the immediate to imagine the age to come. In other words, Jesus is both immanent and transcendent. In the gospel of John, we see this union of Jesus' divinity and humanity. Jesus shows who he is by demonstrating miraculous signs that both meet the needs of the present moment and cast a vision for what is to come. He turns water into wine, making the wedding more festive, and also demonstrating his authority. He heals the royal official's son, a paralytic, a blind man, and raises Lazarus from the dead. He even walks on water and demonstrates his authority over material matters. Jesus is showing us that materially significant *signs* point to his lordship. Our politics serve a similar purpose. How Christians act politically points to a Savior who is leading us.

John 6 shows us this clearly when Jesus feeds the five thousand. In this miracle he demonstrates miraculous abundance and redistribution. He meets the people's immediate needs. This was a sign that Jesus is the Messiah. Yet Jesus tells the crowd who keep following him that being fed is not reason alone to follow him, but rather a sign that points to the true reason. Jesus identifies himself as the bread of life. He says that if we eat of his flesh, we will never go hungry and will have eternal life. That cosmic eternal hope motivates our political action today. Because we have partaken in the bread of life, we have sustenance to endure the difficulty of political progress.

The spiritual component of our political engagement is essential to our work. We need metaphysical hope because the forces we are up against are so vast, and the tools we have to fight them are so weak. We will often feel like David fighting Goliath: outmatched and ready to be made into a mockery. But God uses the lowly and the weak to overtake the strong. That promise is a gift to those who believe, and we can share that gift in the cold, calculated, and cynical field of politics.

Our political participation, as followers of God, is a seed of hope for those who are downtrodden and despairing over the limitations of our political arrangement. Our hope overflows and gives hope to others so that we are not beaten down by the brutality of politics, but rather endure through it because we follow the One whose love endures forever, and who promises that we too will endure forever.

We then can take the side of the oppressed, the side Jesus takes, knowing that full liberation awaits us in the age to come. The last will be first, and the first last. The valleys will be filled, and the hills lowered. All wrongs will be made rights. Because of that enduring promise, we can share anger with the oppressed, and share hope with them too, as we continue to be moved by Jesus to embrace the political demands of the gospel.

Acknowledgments

I have so many people to thank for this book. What an experience and joy it has been to embark on this journey. Thank you to Herald Press and the stellar team there: to Laura Leonard for finding me and believing in me, to Aly Bennett Smith for helping promote the book and being a great Twitter mutual, and to Amy Gingerich for supporting me throughout the process. Y'all rock, and I'm so grateful for you.

Thanks to Kristen Rashid, my dear wife, who talked me through the process, helped me write a great proposal, and edited each chapter before I submitted them. She put in hours of work, and I am eternally grateful. And to Elaine and Agatha, my two sweet daughters, who learned what it was like to relate to a dad who was typing away on Saturday mornings. Thanks for your love and patience, girls.

Thanks to Circle of Hope and their leaders, who affirmed me in this work and supported me throughout this project. Tricia Fussaro was a tremendous gift to me during the writing process, while she was also doing incredibly heavy lifting for the church. I owe you a debt. Andrea McIntosh was a special support to me, and like a sister; as a third-culture kid, we shared in so much camaraderie. Hana Lehmann, Matthew

Abraham, Robert Buck, Corinne Bergmann, Jimmy Weitzel, and Tessa Patino were leaders who affirmed this project. Wes Willison, Megan Jackson, Jordan Burdge, Kristen Snow, and Bryant Burkhart helped shape it from the start—you are all so brilliant. My sister Bethany Stewart was an ally and inspiration throughout; Julie Hoke, one of our pastors, was very loving in the process. Thanks to Israel Vazquez, who took my headshots. I am also very grateful for my cell during this time, including Mark Netti, Lauren Dye Netti, Sean Pepley, Dani Morsberger, Laura Villenueve, and Luke Myers. Special thanks to my political junkie friend, Bethany Bender, who always has the insight of a Beltway insider and who likes my esoteric tweets about politics.

I am deeply grateful for the r/Christianity subreddit ecosystem in general, but especially Bryan and Brandon Peach for their listening ears and incredible writing advice, Jordan Blythe for his promo material, David Coulter for your general brilliance and wisdom, Kristy Burmeister for the solidarity and advice about publishing, Ken Myers for the book writing advice, Stan Patton for the bit about pineapple pizza, Jonathan Balmer for that copy of *Crucifixion* you sent me after we argued about the cross, Sara Little for your support and encouragement, Jacob May for your incredible politics, Jake Raabe for publishing advice, Tim Callow for the chats, especially about Romans 13, Hannah Lee for inspiring Dante in the intro, Nathan Nixon for help with the headshot, and last but not least, Sara Jane Nixon, a favorite person and friend. Not to mention the Twitter group chat that spawned from that community: Brian Lomax (who read large portions throughout the writing process from his post in the Department of Transporation—shout-out to Pete Buttigieg, too), Aaron Foltz,

Doug Chu, Christopher Johnson, Jake Raabe, David Kamphius, David Jacob, and Paul Neusch.

I also wouldn't be here without the sage wisdom of Melissa Florer-Bixler, Drew Hart, Shane Claiborne, and Eliza Griswold. Special thanks to Matt Thiessen for his scholarly review of the book.

I have to acknowledge my seminary professors who prepared me for this moment: Donald Brash, Debbie Watson, Debbie Winters, and Diane Chen.

And for all the readers and Twitter mutuals who are reading this, thank you so much. I'm filled with gratitude for your support.

Notes

INTRODUCTION

1. Dante Alighieri, *The Divine Comedy of Dante Alighieri: The Italian Text with a Translation in English and Commentary*, trans. Courtney Langdon (Cambridge, MA: Harvard University Press, 1918), https://oll.libertyfund .org/title/langdon-the-divine-comedy-vol-1-inferno-english-trans#lf0045-01 _head_006.

CHAPTER 1

1. In the Bible the term *love feast* is used once, in Jude 12, where Jude is telling his audience that their love feasts are corrupted by self-centered, disrespectful people. In 1 Corinthians 11:17–34, Paul admonishes the community for having love feasts that are centered on individuals, and lack the communitarian, egalitarian quality of the first days of the Christian church as described in Acts 2.

2. Executive Office of the President, Executive Order, "Protecting the Nation from Foreign Terrorist Entry into the United States," 82 FR 8977, 8977–8982 (January 27, 2017).

3. Michelle Ye Hee Lee, "Donald Trump's False Comments Connecting Mexican Immigrants and Crime," *Washington Post*, July 8, 2015, https://www.washingtonpost.com/news/fact-checker/wp/2015/07/08/ donald-trumps-false-comments-connecting-mexican-immigrants-and-crime/.

4. Jessica Martínez and Gregory A. Smith, "How the Faithful Voted: A Preliminary 2016 Analysis," Pew Research Center, November 9, 2016, https://www.pewresearch.org/fact-tank/2016/11/09/ how-the-faithful-voted-a-preliminary-2016-analysis/.

5. Donald J. Trump, "The Inaugural Address," January 20, 2017, Washington, D.C., https://trumpwhitehouse.archives.gov/briefings-statements/the-inaugural-address/.

6. Fleming Rutledge, *Crucifixion* (Grand Rapids, MI: Eerdmans, 2015), 133–134.

7. Julie Hirschfeld Davis, "Trump Calls Some Unauthorized Immigrants 'Animals' in Rant," *New York Times*, May 16, 2018, https://www.nytimes.com/2018/05/16/us/politics/trump-undocumented-immigrants-animals.html.

8. Katie Rogers and Nicholas Fandos, "Trump Tells Congresswomen to 'Go Back' to the Countries They Came From," *New York Times*, July 14, 2019, https://www.nytimes.com/2019/07/14/us/politics/trump-twitter-squad-congress.html.

9. Josh Dawsey. "Trump Derides Protections for Immigrants from 'Shithole' Countries," *The Washington Post*, January 12, 2018, https://www.washingtonpost.com/politics/trump-attacks-protections-for-immigrants-from-shithole-countries-in-oval-office-meeting/2018/01/11/bfc0725c-f711-11e7-91af-31ac729add94_story.html.

10. Azmia Magane, "Obama's Drone Warfare Is Something We Need to Talk About," *Teen Vogue*, June 2, 2017, https://www.teenvogue.com/story/obamas-drone-warfare-is-something-we-need-to-talk-about.

CHAPTER 2

1. James Cone, *God of the Oppressed* (Maryknoll, NY: Orbis, 1997), p. 128.

2. Ibid.

3. James Cone, *A Black Theology of Liberation* (Maryknoll, NY: Orbis, 2010), p. 119–120.

4. Howard Thurman, *Jesus and The Disinherited* (Boston: Beacon Press: 1996), xix.

5. Ibid, 5–8.

6. Stanley Hauerwas, *After Christendom* (Nashville, TN: Abingdon Press: 1991), 7.

7. Stanley Hauerwas, "The Politics of the Church and the Humanity of God," ABC Religion & Ethics, June 19, 2012, https://www.abc.net.au/religion/the-politics-of-the-church-and-the-humanity-of-god/10100464.

8. Ibid.

9. Ibid.

10. Here, Hauerwas and Cone agree. They are both "theocrats" in this sense.

11. Cone, *Black Theology of Liberation*, 129.

12. A womanist is a Black feminist.

13. Delores Williams, *Sisters in the Wilderness* (Maryknoll, NY: Orbis, 2013), 18–19.

14. Ibid., 21.

15. Ibid., 25.
16. Ibid., 27.
17. Ibid., 30

CHAPTER 3

1. Drew Hart, *Who Will Be A Witness?* (Harrisonburg, VA: Herald Press, 2020), 269–270.
2. Ibid., 272.

CHAPTER 4

1. Kevin Schaul, Kate Rabinowitz, and Ted Mellnik, "2020 Turnout Is the Highest in Over a Century," *Washington Post*, November 5, 2020, https://www.washingtonpost.com/graphics/2020/elections/voter-turnout/.
2. Timothy B. Lee, "This video of Ronald Reagan shows how much the Republican Party has changed on immigration," *Vox*, Jan. 29, 2017, https://www.vox.com/2017/1/29/14429368/reagan-bush-immigration-attitude
3. Christi Parsons and Lisa Mascaro, "Obama, Who Sought to Ease Partisanship, Saw It Worsen Instead," *Los Angeles Times*, January 14, 2017, https://www.latimes.com/projects/la-na-pol-obama-partisan/.
4. "Obama Explains How America Went from 'Yes We Can' to 'MAGA'," The Ezra Klein Show, *New York Times*, June 1, 2021, https://www.nytimes.com/2021/06/01/opinion/ezra-klein-podcast-barack-obama.html.
5. Bobby Allyn, "Death Toll in West Texas Shooting Rampage Now at 7," *NPR*, September 1, 2019, https://www.npr.org/2019/09/01/756484824/death-toll-from-shootings-in-west-texas-rises-to-eight/.
6. Aubree Eliza Weaver, "O'Rourke on Mass Shootings: 'Yes, This Is F---ed Up," *Politico*, September 1, 2019, https://www.politico.com/story/2019/09/01/beto-orourke-mass-shootings-fword-1479441.
7. Emma Green, "How Will the Church Reckon with Charlottesville?," *The Atlantic*, August 13, 2017, https://www.theatlantic.com/politics/archive/2017/08/will-the-church-reckon-with-charlottesville/536718/.
8. Abraham Joshua Heschel, *The Prophets: Book Two* (Peabody, MA: Hedrickson Publishers, 1962), 89.

CHAPTER 5

1. Melissa Florer-Bixler, *How To Have An Enemy* (Harrisonburg, VA: Herald Press, 2021), p. 24.
2. Ibid, p. 28.
3. Another name for Satan.
4. Howard Thurman, *Jesus and The Disinherited* (Boston: Beacon Press: 1996), 62–63.

5. DeNeen L. Brown, "'I Am a Man': The Ugly Memphis Sanitation Workers' Strike That Led to MLK's Assassination," *Washington Post,* February 12, 2018, https://www.washingtonpost.com/news/retropolis/wp/2018/02/12/i-am-a-man-the-1968-memphis-sanitation-workers-strike-that-led-to-mlks-assassination/.

6. Ibid.

7. Martin Luther King Jr., "I've Seen The Promised Land," *A Testament of Hope*, ed. James M. Washington (New York City, 1986: HarperOne), p. 286.

8. Linley Sanders, "Nine in Ten Americans Have a Positive View of Martin Luther King Jr.," *YouGov*, January 14, 2021, https://today.yougov.com/topics/politics/articles-reports/2021/01/14/positive-view-martin-luther-king-jr.

9. For more about how alms cleanse Cornelius, see Timothy Reardon's essay "Cleansing through Almsgiving in Luke-Acts: Purity, Cornelius, and the Translation of Acts 15:9," Catholic Biblical Quarterly, July 2016.

10. Colossians 4:10 and 2 Timothy 4:11 make it seem like Mark, the cousin of Barnabas, and Paul eventually reconcile.

11. Florer-Bixler, 146.

CHAPTER 6

1. Justin Lee, *Torn: Rescuing the Gospel from the Gays-vs.-Christians Debate* (New York: Jericho Books, 2012), p. 222.

2. Ryan Briggs, "Circle of Hope Church Comes under Fire for Silencing Gay Congregants," *My City Paper New York City*, November 27, 2013, https://mycitypaper.com/News/Circle-of-Hope-church-comes-under-fire-for-silencing-gay-congregants/.

3. Anne Harding, "Religious Faith Linked to Suicidal Behavior in LGBQ Adults," *Reuters*, April 13, 2018, https://www.reuters.com/article/us-health-lgbq-religion-suicide/religious-faith-linked-to-suicidal-behavior-in-lgbq-adults-idUSKBN1HK2MA.

4. C.S. Lewis, "The Great Divorce," New York, NY: MacMillan Publishing Company, 1946, 31.

5. Aja Romano, "A History of 'Wokeness'," *Vox*, Oct. 9, 2020, https://www.vox.com/culture/21437879/stay-woke-wokeness-history-origin-evolution-controversy.

6. Ibid.

7. David Brooks, "America Is Facing 5 Epic Crises All at Once," *New York Times*, June 25, 2020, https://www.nytimes.com/2020/06/25/opinion/us-coronavirus-protests.html.

8. Bret Stephens, "Woke Me When It's Over", *New York Times*, Feb. 22, 2021, https://www.nytimes.com/2021/02/22/opinion/bon-appetit-cancel-culture.html.

9. Ross Douthat, "When Wokeness Becomes Weakness," *New York Times,* May 1, 2021, https://www.nytimes.com/2021/05/01/opinion/democrats-james-carville.html.

10. Rod Dreher, "Why Are Conservatives In Despair?," *American Conservative,* April 23, 2021, https://www.theamericanconservative.com/dreher/why-are-conservatives-in-despair/.

11. Danté Stewart, Twitter post, March 27, 2021, 11:49am, https://twitter.com/stewartdantec/status/1375837490213441541.

CHAPTER 7

1. The NRSV uses the word *slave* for the Greek verb *edoulōsa* (ἐδούλωσα), which means to become a *doulos* (δοῦλος), but *servant* functions equally well, and doesn't carry the modern baggage of racialized chattel slavery, which I think distracts from the posture of humility Paul is trying to exhibit, and instead reinforces patterns of oppression.

2. Martin Luther King Jr., "Letter from a Birmingham City Jail," *A Testament of Hope,* ed. James M. Washington (New York City: HarperOne, 1986), p. 295.

3. Thomas L. Friedman, "Want to Get Trump Re-elected? Dismantle the Police," *New York Times,* June 22, 2021, https://www.nytimes.com/2021/06/22/opinion/gop-democrats-defund-police-voting.html.

4. Weihua Li and Ilica Mahajan, "Police Say Demoralized Officers Are Quitting In Droves. Labor Data Says No," *The Marshall Project,* September 1, 2021, https://www.themarshallproject.org/2021/09/01/police-say-demoralized-officers-are-quitting-in-droves-labor-data-says-no.

5. Deja Thomas and Juliana Menasce Horowitz, "Support for Black Lives Matter Has Decreased Since June but Remains Strong among Black Americans," *Pew Research Center,* September 16, 2020, https://www.pewresearch.org/fact-tank/2020/09/16/support-for-black-lives-matter-has-decreased-since-june-but-remains-strong-among-black-americans/.

6. Alex Samuels, "How Views on Black Lives Matter Have Changed—and Why That Makes Police Reform So Hard," *FiveThirtyEight,* April 13, 2021, https://fivethirtyeight.com/features/how-views-on-black-lives-matter-have-changed-and-why-that-makes-police-reform-so-hard/.

CHAPTER 8

1. Greg Boyd, Twitter post, August 28, 2020, 11:38am, https://twitter.com/greg_boyd/status/1299385898631598081.

2. Lisa Friedman and Coral Davenport, "Manchin Rejects Landmark Legislation, Putting Biden's Climate Goals at Risk,: *New York Times,* Dec. 19, 2021, https://www.nytimes.com/2021/12/19/climate/manchin-climate-build-back-better-bill.html?searchResultPosition=5.

3. Jonathan Weisman, "In Voting Rights Fight, Democrats Train Ire on Sinema and Manchin," *New York Times*, Jan 19, 2022, https://www .nytimes.com/2022/01/19/us/politics/democrats-filibuster-sinema-manchin .html?searchResultPosition=1.

4. Samuel Haselby, "Divided we stand: The problem with bipartisanship," *Boston.com*, March 22, 2009, http://archive.boston.com/bostonglobe/ideas/ articles/2009/03/22/divided_we_stand/

5. Haselby.

6. *Ant.* 18.1.6.

7. Flavius Joseph, *The Works of Josephus*, trans. William Whiston (Peabody, MA: Hendrickson Publishers, 1987), 477.

8. Anthony J. Saldarini, "Pharisees," *Anchor Bible Dictionary* 5:389.

9. Ibid.

10. Mark L. Strauss, *Four Portraits, One Jesus* (Grand Rapids, MI: Zondervan, 2007), 131–133.

11. Schiffman, Lawrence, "Pharisees," "The Jewish Annotated New Testament," ed. Amy-Jill Levine and Marc Zvi Brettler (New York: Oxford University Press: 271), 619.

12. Karl Barth, *Church Dogmatics, Vol. II: The Doctrine of God, Part 1*, eds. G. W. Bromily and T. F. Torrance, trans. T. H. L. Parker, W. B. Johnston, Harold Knight, and J. L. M. Haire (New York: T&T Clark, 1957, repr. Peabody: Hendrickson Publishers, 2010), 386.

CHAPTER 9

1. Alec Loganbill, "Encountering Race, Creating Place, and Opening Space in the Hardings' Mennonite House," *Anabaptist Historians*, July 30, 2020, https://anabaptisthistorians.org/2020/07/30/encountering-race-creating- place-and-opening-space-in-the-hardings-mennonite-house/.

2. Wikipedia, "Reasonable Suspicion," https://en.wikipedia.org/w/index .php?title=Reasonable_suspicion&oldid=1028783206 (accessed September 11, 2021).

3. Adam Peck, "Mayor Bloomberg: NYPD 'Stops Whites Too Much and Minorities Too Little'," *Think Progress*, June 28, 2013, https:// thinkprogress.org/mayor-bloomberg-nypd-stops-whites-too-much-and- minorities-too-little-7977f5c3436a/.

4. Ibid.

CHAPTER 10

1. Walter Brueggemann, *The Prophetic Imagination* (Minneapolis: Fortress Press, 2001), 45.

2. Ibid., 21.

3. Ibid., 3.

4. Ibid., 22.
5. Ibid., 23.
6. Ibid., 101.
7. Ibid., 82–83
8. Ibid., 94.
9. Ibid., 101–119.
10. Abraham Joshua Heschel, *The Prophets: Book One* (Peabody, MA: Hendrickson Publishers, 1962), 212.
11. Ibid., 219.
12. Ibid.
13. Martin Luther King Jr., "Martin Luther King Jr. saw three evils in the world," The Atlantic, March 2018, https://www.theatlantic.com/magazine/archive/2018/02/martin-luther-king-hungry-club-forum/552533/.
14. George Monbiot, "Neoliberalism—The Ideology at the Root of All Our Problems," *The Guardian*, April 15, 2016, https://www.theguardian.com/books/2016/apr/15/neoliberalism-ideology-problem-george-monbiot.
15. Nathan Robinson, "How Neoliberalism Worms Its Way into Your Brain," *Current Affairs*, April 18, 2018, https://www.currentaffairs.org/2018/04/how-neoliberalism-worms-its-way-into-your-brain.
16. The Greek term here is *dikaiosynēn* (δικαιοσύνην), which can be translated as justice or righteousness.
17. Katie Van Syckle, "In Climate Coverage, Reporting the Grim Facts, but Also the Fight," *New York Times,* August 27, 2021, https://www.nytimes.com/2021/08/27/insider/united-nations-climate-report.html.
18. Willie Jennings, "Overcoming Racial Bias," *Divinity*, Duke University, Spring 2015, p. 5–9.
19. John Gramlich, "The Gap Between the Number of Blacks and Whites in Prison Is Shrinking," *Pew Research Center*, April 30, 2019.
20. Li Zhou, "Where Americans Stand on Policing Today," *Vox*, April 9, 2021, https://www.vox.com/22372342/police-reform-derek-chauvin.
21. Jacques Ellul, *Violence: Reflections from a Christian Perspective*, trans. Cecelia Gaul Kings (Eugene, OR: Wipf and Stock, 1969), 84.
22. Ibid., 22.
23. Ibid., 88.
24. Ibid., 93.
25. Gillian Brockell, "She Was the Only Member of Congress to Vote Against War in Afghanistan. Some Called Her a Traitor," *Washington Post*, August 17, 2021, https://www.washingtonpost.com/history/2021/08/17/barbara-lee-afghanistan-vote/.
26. William Cavanaugh, *Migrations of the Holy* (Grand Rapids, MI: Eerdmans, 2011), 45.
27. Daniel Bell, *The Economy of Desire* (Grand Rapids, MI: Baker, 2012), 39.

CHAPTER 11

1. Gregory A., Smith, "More White Americans Adopted Than Shed Evangelical Label During Trump Presidency, Especially His Supporters," *Pew Research Center*, September 15, 2021, https://www.pewresearch .org/fact-tank/2021/09/15/more-white-americans-adopted-than-shed-evangelical-label-during-trump-presidency-especially-his-supporters/.

2. Robert Jewett, *Romans: A Commentary*, Hermeneia Bible Commentary, ed. Eldon J. Epp (Minneapolis: Fortress Press, 2007), 289.

3. Karl Barth, *The Epistle To The Romans* (London: Oxford University Press: 1968), 484.

4. Jewett, 289.

5. Ibid., 290.

6. Gerhard Kittle, Bromiley, Gerhard Friedrich, and Ronald E. Pitkin, *Theological dictionary of the New Testament VIII.* (Grand Rapids, Mich: Eerdmans: 1965), 29.

7. Walter Bauer, "A Greek-English Lexicon of the New Testament and Other Early Christian Literature," translated by William F. Ardnt and F. Wilbur Hingrich, (Chicago: University of Chicago Press, 1979), 805.

8. N.T. Wright, *The Kingdom New Testament* (New York: HarperOne, 2011), 332.

9. David Bentley Hart, *The New Testament: A Translation* (New Haven, CT: Yale University Press, 2017), 312.

10. Amy-Jill Levine, *The Jewish Annotated New Testament*, ed. Amy-Jill Levine and Marc Zvi Brettler (New York: Oxford University Press: 271), 314.

CHAPTER 12

1. Willie Jennings, "My Anger, God's Righteous Indignation," interview by Evan Rosa, *For the Life of the World*, Yale Center for Faith & Culture, June 2, 2020, https://for-the-life-of-the-world-yale-center-for-faith-culture.simplecast.com/episodes/my-anger-gods-righteous-indignation-willie-jennings-response-to-the-death-of-george-floyd-FXkkWh9b/ transcript.

2. Bruxy Cavey, "God Hates Religion: Interview with Bruxy Cavey on the End of Religion," interview by Jonny Rashid, *Restore and Restore: a spiritual life podcast*, July 1, 2021, https://www.circleofhope.church/ blog/god-hates-religion-interview-with-bruxy-cavey-on-the-end-of-religion-ep-35/.

3. Jennings, "My Anger."

4. Osheta Moore, *Dear White Peacemakers* (Harrisonburg, VA: Herald Press, 2021), 138.

5. Michael D. Shear, "Trump and Aides Drove Family Separation at Border, Documents Say," *New York Times*, Jan. 14, 2021, https://www.nytimes .com/2021/01/14/us/politics/trump-family-separation.html.

About the Author

Jonny Rashid has served as pastor for Circle of Hope, a cell church in Philadelphia, for over ten years. He is father to Elaine and Agatha, and married to Kristen. He lives on Lenape land, colonized as Philadelphia, in the northern part of the city. Jonny moved to Philadelphia from Lebanon, Pennsylvania, where his parents emigrated to from Egypt. He studied journalism and history at Temple University and completed his Master of Divinity at Palmer Theological Seminary.

Photo by Israel Vasquez